Happy Lawyer
Happy Life

The Cataloguing-in-Publication entry for this book is available with the National Library of Australia
Creator: Rayward, Clarissa, author.
Title: Happy Lawyer Happy Life: How to be happy in law and in life
ISBN: 978-0-9942025-2-9 (pbk)

Printed in Australia by Excite Print
Text design by Lauren Jennings, Graphic Designer, Brisbane
Cover design by Lauren Jennings and Sarah Follent, Brisbane
Cover image by Marshall Rees, Photographer, Brisbane
Cover hair by Jools Purchase, Stylist, Brisbane
Cover makeup by Bethany Prickett, Make-up Artist, Brisbane
Editing by Grammar Factory

Disclaimer

The material in this publication is of the nature of general comment only, and does not represent professional advice. It is not intended to provide specific guidance for particular circumstances and it should not be relied on as the basis for any decision to take action or not take action on any matter which it covers. Readers should obtain professional advice where appropriate, before making any such decision. To the maximum extent permitted by law, the author and publisher disclaim all responsibility and liability to any person, arising directly or indirectly from any person taking or not taking action based on the information in this publication.

Happy Lawyer Happy Life

HOW TO BE HAPPY IN LAW AND LIFE

CLARISSA RAYWARD

Contents

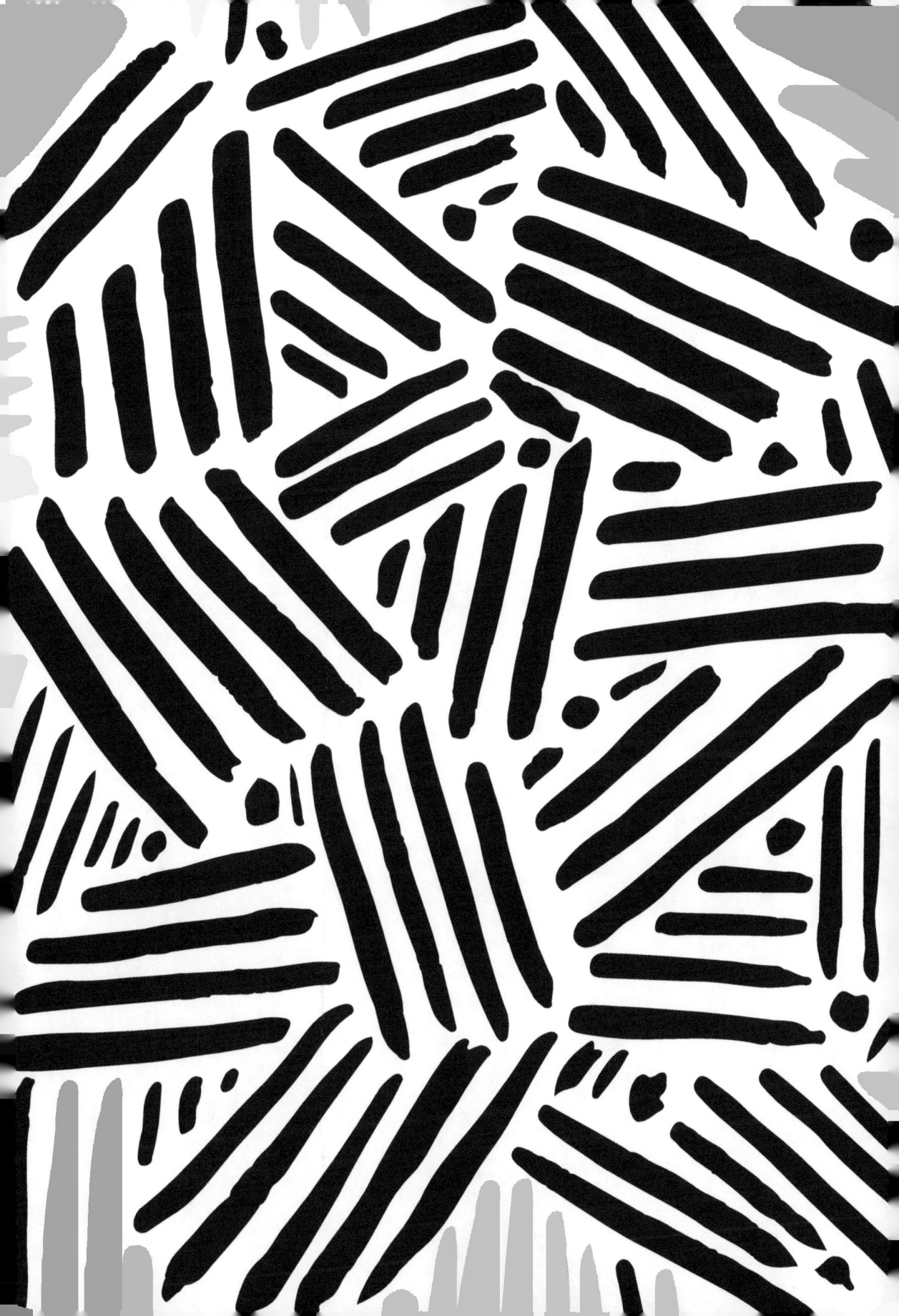

INTRODUCTION

To live a life with purpose.

To say the courageous thing.

To celebrate the simple gift.

To follow your dreams.

This is a happy life.

– WAYLAND HENRY –

Introduction

I have never regretted my decision to study law. But I have often regretted the impact that I have allowed the practice of law to have on my life. It is this sense of regret, which I have come to accept, understand and manage, that has inspired this book.

There have been many moments in my career when I have considered throwing in the law towel. Mostly those moments arise when I am feeling tired, overwhelmed and unappreciated, those times in life when I have felt I have given everything to my job and my career, to the detriment of myself.

Being a lawyer, working in law and loving the many lawyers who are my friends, I have come to accept that this career comes with ups and downs, highs and lows, successes and lessons. But find me a career that doesn't. When it comes to being unhappy in this or any profession, I have realised that we cannot place the blame so easily – we put too much pressure on our jobs, our employers and our relationships to make us happy when, really, it is up to us.

In sharing the story of my pursuit of happiness in law (and in life), I want to be clear from the outset – I don't profess to have all the answers. These pages contain my learnings – from my own experience, from the sidelines observing the experiences of others, from much reading and from talking to many lawyers about their happiness or lack thereof.

But what does it even mean to be 'happy'?

Happiness is different for all of us. However, there are some common themes – a sense of belonging, purpose and meaning. A feeling of contentment, pleasure and joy.

Your happiness and my happiness might be different, and the beautiful thing about the world is that this is more than okay – what makes you 'you' will be different from what makes me 'me'. We may have some similarities and perhaps many differences. But I expect, if you are reading this, you will know a lawyer, be thinking of becoming a lawyer, or actually be a lawyer, so we have that in common if nothing else.

WHY ARE LAWYERS SO UNHAPPY?

The purpose of this book is to focus on how we find and maintain happiness, but I think it is important to touch on the topics that keep coming up when unhappiness is discussed in relation to lawyers.

I have read a lot of studies telling us what makes lawyers unhappy (and believe me, there is plenty written on this) – enough to let you in on the key factors that lie beneath this unfortunate trend.

It seems to be bundled into these six categories:

Natural pessimism

It seems that many of us were born with the innate ability to find everything wrong with any situation. This skill is honed at law school and exploited in the traditional practice of law.

We are often critical of the lack of useful teaching at law school when it comes to working as a lawyer, but one thing I think law school does teach us is the capacity to think 'like a lawyer'. This tends to mean we accept nothing at face value, question everything and are encouraged to look for all of the possible risks, problems or challenges to ensure we have prepared our case for all eventualities.

A study conducted in 2000, 'Countering Lawyer Unhappiness: Pessimism, Decision Latitude and the Zero-Sum Dilemma' [1] found that law students who were naturally pessimistic performed better at law school than students who were more naturally optimistic. The study concluded that a pessimistic lawyer is perhaps a good thing for society but not such a good thing for us individual lawyers.

Sadly, our pessimism tends to extend beyond the analysis of a client contract to the interpretation of our own lives. Often, we don't just see the bad in a situation – we only see the bad, as if there is never any good. Unsurprisingly, pessimism and unhappiness are related, and so this is the beginning of the 'unhappy lawyer'.

---

1   'Countering Lawyer Unhappiness: Pessimism, Decision Latitude and the Zero-Sum Dilemma' Paul R Verkuil, Cardozo Law School, Martin Seligman, University of Pennsylvania, Department of Psychology and Terry Kang. http://papers.ssrn.com/sol3/papers.cfm?abstract_id=241942

The nature of the beast

Most lawyers in traditional firms are spending their days getting other people out of some sort of chaos, conflict or debacle, which is rarely pleasant. Let's be frank, most of us don't consult with lawyers when life is going great. Usually, something unexpected, untoward or downright terrible has occurred, and the lawyer is the person we turn to in the hope they can get us out of the mess, and fast. I often describe my role in traditional or litigation practice in this way:

Imagine you are on the hospital operating table. Around you is a team of amazing surgeons, doctors and nurses doing all they can to fix you, but at the same time, there is an equally talented group doing everything they can to undo the good work of the first team to ensure that you don't survive.

In its coldest, simplest form, this is the life of a lawyer. While we are doing all we can to save, protect and further the needs of our client, our opponents are actively doing the opposite. It is like a battlefield that keeps the contestants in a heightened state of stress the whole time the game is going on. And for most lawyers, no sooner has one game successfully concluded than another begins, so that heightened stress never really goes away. Most lawyers spend their days working under immense pressure, where the stakes are high. For most of us, this style of work doesn't fuel happiness.

Tradition and career progression

Law has been around for so long, it is hard to work out when it really began. And many of the traditions our profession still observes today feel, at times, like they could have ended a good 100 or more years ago. Law is very slow to change. And it is this unwillingness to move quickly with the times that fuels much of the unhappiness of those practising within it. A simple and good example of this is timesheets.

Despite much discussion, for many years, about the need to do away with timesheets, it is still the case for most of us that our daily worth is neatly summarised in six-minute units on a spreadsheet. The pressure to record each minute of each day in some billable way is something even I have struggled to let go of, despite the fact I would be seen as one of the more progressive of my kind. I still occasionally catch myself thinking, 'Well, you haven't done much billable work today, so you should probably take that file home.'

I don't know of many other workplaces (except perhaps accountants, as I sense we are the same on this one) where 'billable' and 'non-billable' work tasks are so clearly identified and separated. And what happens when you are set a daily target of, say, 6.5 'billable' hours is that you spend your day trying to find just that – 6.5 (or seven or even eight) BILLABLE hours.

That statement in itself has to be the death of all possible creativity and innovation. The idea that a lawyer could sit, ponder and dream an impossible dream will never fall into the box of billable time (unless, perhaps, it is a dream to solve a client's legal problem in a completely new but billable way). Once you have seen your worth mapped out on a spreadsheet for a few years, it is very hard to let go of that. And when those numbers don't add up to much, it is not long before your own sense of personal worth looks about as attractive as your 'actual billed time'.

Exacerbating this challenge is the fact that much of the traditional career progression in larger law firms is aligned with a lawyer's capacity to maximise their billable time. To become an associate and later a partner, you need to be able to clearly demonstrate your worth to your organisation. There is no better way than by maximising your billable worth. This means long hours, and prioritising billable activity over the unrecognised, non-billable tasks such as customer service, mentoring, marketing, reading and learning.

I have seen friends having to account for almost every minute of their day using fancy software designed to maximise productivity thanks to its capacity to accurately calculate the time you spent having bathroom breaks during the day. And then there are those 'perks' of the big firms – from in-house meals, particularly after hours, to taxi vouchers to get you home. These alleged perks are built into the work environment as a great benefit, but they only reinforce a culture of overworking.

Personality types

Law is full of A-type personalities – high achievers who are some of the most intelligent people you will find. And when we think of lawyers, there are a bundle of social stereotypes that roll off the tongue, 'sharks' and 'hired guns' being my favourites. But even if we ignore the extremes, I can safely say that, as a lawyer, you learn pretty early on that you cannot be seen to be 'weak'. Sadly, kindness, generosity and empathy are traits mistaken by many as a sign of weakness, particularly when it comes to lawyers. So, very early in their careers, most lawyers create a hard exterior that is never dropped. Some will even be openly aggressive, bullish and unkind, all in an attempt to maintain a facade of strength and power.

But what of the lawyer who, at heart, is kind? Who is not aggressive, and is focused on the task at hand rather than the need to be seen in a particular way to maintain a stereotype created by 1980s TV dramas?

As more and more women have flooded our profession these past years, the stereotypes of what it means to be a lawyer are being heavily challenged. When I think of the best barristers and litigators I know, they are anything but 'sharks'. They don't lurk in the shadows – they do anything but. They swim with their clients in the shallow waters, supporting them, sharing the load and guiding them down a well-chosen path. They are great at their jobs, and they use compassion, creativity, understanding and deep legal knowledge – traits that are anything but shark-like.

I don't get to court too much any more, but when I do, I always enjoy a bit of 'lawyer gazing'. It intrigues me to see how two colleagues who are otherwise great friends can quickly get drawn into heated and frivolous conversations about who has the best case. The whole time, the clients are watching. In contrast, those lawyers I see who are truly at the top of their game are calm and respectful, and often say very little about their case to their opponent. They stand back and take in the scene, actively listening to the conversation occurring around them. That, to me, is the sign of a great lawyer –calm under fire, compassionate and curious.

But while I may think that these are the traits that ultimately make for a great lawyer, the sad truth is that there are many still who disagree. And so law firms, courts, litigation and negotiations are often full of more stereotypical lawyer 'sharks', who are easy to associate with those old-school lawyer stereotypes.

The profession is changing and so are the expectations of just what it takes to be a great lawyer. But that change is slow, and there is no doubt that those of us who have had to work with those 'lawyer sharks' – the ones that are lurking in the office shadows waiting to take advantage of any small sign of weakness, have felt the unhappiness that they seem so able to create.

The work itself

I must say that when I bounced off to law school, I did so with visions of saving the wrongly accused from a life behind bars. I even had moments when I thought I would spend my days as a 'proper lawyer' just as Erin Brockovich had – sneaking around government departments or commercial job sites, saving the local residents from certain harm. At one stage, I envisioned myself working within the United Nations, saving the world from war criminals.

And then I got a job. In a real law firm. Practising criminal law. I had visions of Law and Order for about the first five minutes of the first day before I realised that most of the clients I dealt with were destined for jail – and for good reason.

Even so, I was lucky to have started my job in the law when there were jobs to be had. Now there are so few jobs for the huge numbers of graduates being pumped out of our universities that I am seeing students applying in large numbers for any job a law firm has to offer.

For most law graduates, their days in law begin in medium or large law firms, full of structure, rules and traditions. And for these lawyers, there are often many billable hours spent doing tasks that are anything but exciting, fast-paced or interesting. Instead, days will often be spent at a single desk on tedious tasks over which that lawyer has almost no control. They are unlikely to find themselves sitting with a client for many months. And they will probably be one piece in a much larger puzzle of solicitors, junior and senior associates, special counsel and partners. Certainly not the life of Erin Brockovich. There's no real chance of feeling like you are making a difference in the world when you're editing one paragraph in a 500-page document, ten times each day.

A few months of this might be manageable for some, as long as they can see that light at the end of the hierarchical tunnel. But the difficulty for many of our young lawyers is that they fought hard to be at the top of their game during law school and then beat the odds to score a job at a great firm. Now, when it turns out it is not quite what they had in mind, the idea of looking for something else is surely the ultimate defeat. So they push on. For a few more years. Until it really does feel too late to leave.

Other lawyers

We can't forget the role of other lawyers in our unhappiness. Only last year, I had a senior member of our profession deliberately and openly bully me in court during a trial in which it was my job to represent two children. Comments were made loud enough for all to hear about my actions and what steps might be taken against me personally at the conclusion of the matter. What disappointed me most was not the commentary; it was that a person whom I and many others in our profession respected considered this to be an appropriate tactic to employ in a case that involved the serious issue of violence against children. All because we stood on different sides of the case.

Law is an adversarial system where lawyers are encouraged to act as zealous advocates. Unfortunately, this means that there is a very fine and mobile line between what is deemed 'appropriate advocacy' and what can become heartless, personal or strategic attacks.

The lack of trust between lawyers from different firms is high. While you might accept that others embrace the same ethical standards, you will rarely find a situation where lawyers from opposing offices are willing to trust each other without first having worked extensively together in other matters.

Our modern-day culture of fast-paced online communication is only making the situation worse. I have noticed a shift away from picking up the phone to touch base with a colleague on the other side of a matter to a practice of sending sharp, pointed emails. These are often fired off with little consideration for the recipient – either lawyer or client. And in these days of instantaneous communication, that email that you decided to fire off on Saturday afternoon, because that was when you were catching up on work, arrived in your colleague's inbox right when they were trying to enjoy their son's football match. And now they are livid, because what you hastily wrote is going to send their client into a spin and they know they will have to deal with that on Monday.

It is bad enough to spend your days dealing with a client's conflict. It adds a whole new level of stress and tension when you are not only managing your client, but also have a difficult, abrasive and inconsiderate opponent to deflect as well. And depending on the level of support you have where you work, this experience can quickly become exhausting and isolating, leading, of course, to more and more unhappiness.

There are, no doubt, many more reasons why we lawyers are currently so unhappy. Whatever the cause, once you understand the source of your unhappiness, you can start to address it. Take the unhappy bull by the horns and tackle it!

But where do you start?

CAN LAWYERS REALLY BE HAPPY?

My pursuit of happiness came at a time when I could feel my discontent with my work. I was not waking up and bouncing out of bed to get to the office; I was actively looking for reasons not to have to be there. I was finding myself struggling to do things in my job that I had been doing for years – even the simple stuff was becoming tedious and hard. I was finding myself too easily drawn into discussions about negative experiences, feelings or even gossip. I was spending most of my time worrying, and most of that worry was focused not on what I felt or thought but on what others would think, feel or say about me. I was, in turn, distracted in my marriage, feeling disconnected from my daughter and finding my friendships becoming harder to enjoy. I describe this as me feeling 'unhappy'.

Research the world over is showing us that lawyers are unhappy in very large numbers. Here in Australia, current research suggests one in three of us will experience depression at some stage during our careers. To me, that statistic is overwhelming. And so very sad.

My open and active pursuit of happiness in law came at a time when I was unhappy. I was not depressed. I had not become part of the statistics and am grateful that I was able to work through my unhappiness by myself and come out the other side. I have, however, seen around me the impact of anxiety and depression on colleagues in the law. It is debilitating. And can be fatal.

Much of my reading on unhappiness in law has focused on the very real risks of depression and anxiety. While it is essential that we better understand and manage these serious health conditions, the purpose of this book is to consider those of us in the profession who are not sufferers, but who are perhaps at risk down the track if we don't change our ways now.

Over the past few years, I have seen so many of my friends, colleagues and acquaintances struggle with the stress of a profession they once loved. I have come to conclude this is not a 'stage of life' thing, as I am seeing law students struggle as much as I am seeing successful partners in large organisations question whether this career is still for them. So why were we attracted to this stressful profession in the first place? I have come to conclude that there are two primary reasons we are drawn to law.

Firstly, there is what I call the lawyer stereotype, or the social norms that we have come to associate with lawyers – they are powerful, successful, intelligent and rich. This stereotype, love it or hate it, can open many doors in life.

The second reason, and the area I am more passionate about, is the desire to make a difference in the world. So many great lawyers are driven to law school because they can see that the practice of law will bring them an opportunity to leave a legacy, however big or small. That desire to positively impact the lives of others is the thing that brought me to law school and is still the thing that lets me survive in law practice now. And when it comes to being happy, I can now see with clarity that the minute I allowed my own passion, purpose and legacy be a part of my daily practice of law, I found a renewed energy for my work and, in turn, happiness.

I expect, if you are reading this book, that it was the second of the drivers above that brought you to law. And there is a strong chance that some of the passion and purpose that brought you here – that desire to make a positive difference in the lives of others – has started to fall away. I expect that your work life has become a little blurry, and probably very busy, with so much going on that you can't tell me in detail just what you did today. And there is a good chance that if I asked you to tell me the last time you actually felt like you made a positive difference in the life of another person, you would have to pause, think hard and search back a little way. It probably seems like forever ago that you really felt great in your work.

The thing is, I bet even today (or last Friday, if you are reading this on the weekend!), something you have done at work has had a positive impact in the world – the difficulty right now is that you won't have noticed it. You have not trained your brain to look for and see these moments. Instead, your brain is very focused on what needs to be done, what is on that to-do list, and what you have to get through to make sure you can hit those billable targets. I expect that same brain is the one you take home with you and, sadly, it doesn't come with an off switch. So at home, you probably find you are distracted, worrying about work and planning tomorrow rather than living today.

I can find hundreds of articles on why lawyers are unhappy. But I find so few that tell me how the unhappy lawyer can become happy again. Among those that I have found, many seem to suggest that happiness is found when lawyers leave the practice of the law and follow their passion – their dreams outside of the law. But what about the unhappy lawyer whose passion is the law? What if they don't necessarily want to leave but, rather, want to find happiness in the position that they have worked so many years to achieve, enjoying their life at the same time? Why is that impossible?

The thing is, as a lawyer, an employer, a colleague and a friend, I don't want good lawyers leaving the law! I want my profession to be full of great lawyers – those who are actively leaving a positive mark on the lives of those around them. And I know that for great lawyers to stay in this profession, they will need to find happiness – a sense of purpose, contentment and belonging.

Someone recently challenged me about my constant talk of happiness, suggesting that being happy is unachievable. That is not my experience.

I have found that by choosing my own happiness, looking for the good and being grateful for all that comes my way, but at the same time acknowledging and expecting sadness and disappointment, I have found a way to be happy in almost every moment. This sense of happiness is a daily work in progress – it is not something I have found you can achieve once and then just expect to always have. It requires conscious thought, which, on some days, will be a lot easier than on others. But it is possible.

THE **HAPPY** LAWYER

Throughout this book, I will share with you my learnings on happiness in law. I have had the chance to speak with many other happy lawyers who have shared their experiences also. Hopefully, between all of us, we can find a way to make you happy too. In two parts, this book will help you to explore the possibility of happiness in law and guide you through the practical steps required to make it a reality.

Part One looks at our understanding of happiness. As we know, happiness can mean different things to different people. We will delve into what happiness means to you, before looking at the recent research into the causes and effects of happiness in our brains and bodies.

Part Two addresses how to be a happy lawyer and takes you through the five drivers of happiness in law (and in life):

Health

Attitude

Passion

Purpose

You

A few years ago, I chose to be happy. I chose to stop looking for the bad and find the good. I chose to take my own advice, which I was so willing to hand out to those around me, and, as they say on aeroplanes, 'fit my own mask first'. I didn't have to spend lots of money or head off and do something new, and I didn't have to leave law. I just had to change the way I saw the world. And I am going to encourage you to do the same.

PART ONE:

Happiness is...

Happiness, like unhappiness, - is a - proactive choice.

- STEVEN COVEY -

The meaning of happiness

For me, happiness is the feeling of contentment that comes from living in the present, looking for the good in any situation and being grateful for all things, no matter how challenging.

This might seem a daunting question at first. We can list all of the things that make us unhappy very quickly, but articulating the meaning of true happiness can be a challenge. Luckily, there is an easy way to start. Part of training ourselves to be consistently happy begins with focusing on just what it is that makes us happy right now.

WHAT MAKES YOU HAPPY?

If I had to answer this question today, it would be easy. I am writing my book in a beautiful homestead about two hours from my home. My whole family is here (all of them – parents, brother, nieces and nephews), and they are currently out walking. I am in complete peace, on a beautiful, cold but sunny day, sitting by a fire and doing something I love. Really, it is no surprise that I am having no trouble feeling happy today. My list might look a bit like this:

Clarissa's list of happy things today:

- Got to sleep in until 7am (#winning!).

- Woke up to a stunning view of Mt Barney from my bedroom window.

- Enjoyed my daughter's beautiful smile as she ran off to feed apples to a horse.

- Took my husband a slightly dodgy coffee in bed and found he was genuinely surprised, which made me smile (can you tell I don't do it that often?).

- Had a beautiful breakfast with my daughter and my niece cuddling on my lap because it was so cold.

- Found my mum's stash of homemade gingerbread cookies and gobbled them down.

- Put on my favourite song of the week and danced like no one was watching (because no one was!).

- Managed to sneak out for a short drive to:

    a.   Find internet reception and sneakily check my Instagram.
    b.   Grab a 'proper coffee' so I can survive the day.

- Had a few moments of quiet conversation with my aunt, who is still recovering after my beautiful uncle passed away earlier this year.

I could go on and on. It does, of course, help that it is a Saturday! Had you asked me to answer a question like this yesterday, you would have a very different list.

Yesterday, I was at my desk in my office, madly trying to do about 500 things, with challenges coming left, right and centre – I had staff members who were unwell, technological problems, unhappy clients and a deadline that I was struggling to meet. Yesterday, I was finding it much harder to be happy.

But let's give it a go (just for the fun of it).

Clarissa's list of 'happiness' for yesterday (a not-so-great work day):

- Started the day my favourite way – with my daughter, sitting and chatting in bed in the morning.

- Had a great session at the gym with my daughter- she was hanging from the rings before charging around on her scooter while I was attempting to remain healthy.

- Had my perfect morning coffee, thanks to the girls around the corner.

- Snuck in a 'healthy chocolate smoothie' for brekky!

- Managed to get all my jobs done and make it to the office before 10am. (I had to vote in an election and pack bags for three people to get away for the weekend and it was an achievement to get that done in one-and-a-half hours, let me tell you!)

- Despite the missing team members at work, was made to smile thanks to the great attitude of a few others who filled in the gaps and even brought me lunch.

- Managed to get that MailChimp email formatted and sent despite the constant technical challenges (it only took three hours …).

- Had two-and-a-half hours of fun in the car with my husband and daughter playing 'I spy' and enjoying a Disney sing-along.

- Arrived at our weekend home away from home to enjoy all my nieces and nephews tearing around the house at 100 miles an hour, having the time of their lives.

And the list really could go on! Yesterday was a day determined to try me, but it is interesting what happens when you force your mind to go hunting for the happy, particularly on those tricky days.

Now it's your turn.

What has made me happy today?

Grab a pen and let's answer some questions that will help you get to the core of what happiness is for you.

Just as I did earlier, let's start in the 'right now'. I want you to take the time to pause and do your own brain dump of anything that has made you happy today. It can be big, small, important or not. It doesn't matter. Just jot everything down, the more the merrier. When I make myself do these tasks, I just want the immediate things that come to mind. And I don't want to give myself time to analyse these thoughts – I just want my 'gut feel' answers.

I encourage you to take only a few moments.

1 ....

2 ....

3. ....

4. ....

5. ....

6. ....

7 ....

8 ....

9 ....

10. ....

So now you have a list of what has made you happy today. I hope somewhere on that list are a few small things – a child or partner's smile, a nice coffee in the morning, a beautiful, sunny day... Try to fill the page – you might be surprised what you find!

What has made me happy this week?

You will soon start to see a pattern to these lists (and you have probably already realised that I love lists!). Write down all the things you can think of this past week that have made you feel some sense of happiness.

1   ....

2   ....

3.   ....

4.   ....

5.   ....

6.   ....

7   ....

8   ....

9   ....

10. ....

How are you going? Are you seeing any themes when it comes to what makes you happy? What are they?

What has made me happy this year?

Let's go a bit broader. This time, cast your mind back a little further and write down all the things you can immediately think of that have made you happy in the past year. Take a look at the date right now and then take yourself back to this very day last year (feel free to open your calendar – it will tell you exactly what was happening). Work your way through each week and each month and give me the biggest list possible of all the things that have made you feel happy. Here's my example:

Clarissa's list of 'happiness' for this past year

- Our recent family holiday to New Zealand – so beautiful, such fun and we did it last year too, so it is becoming a wonderful August tradition.

- Launching my podcast – something I have been working on for a long time and it made it to the airwaves just last week!

- My friendships – this could take up many bullet points. So many of my friends, who support me, and share their lives and themselves, are off chasing dreams. They have brought so much happiness to my life this past year.

- My family – all of them (even the annoying ones) bring a smile to my face.

- My daughter – she has made the transition to kindergarten happily and is growing into a gorgeous, curious person who makes me smile every day.

- Award nominations – I know it sounds cheesy, but it is nice to have your hard work recognised. This year, there have been a few awards that I was really proud to receive.

- My return to fitness and health – this has really brought me happiness this year. I focused on making my own health a priority and I have done it.

My list could and will go on … I just won't put it all in this book or you will be very bored! It's your turn again. Take the opportunity to grab some snacks – this list might take some time!

1 ....

2 ....

3. ....

4. ....

5. ....

6. ....

7 ....

8 ....

9 ....

10. ....

So what did you find was different about your list for the past year, compared to your list for this past week?

I know when I did this and went back over the past year, there were a great many things that I could say made me feel happy, but they tended to be those bigger things – holidays, events, awards, parties, achievements … there were fewer of those small moments, the ones that are captured when I do the same exercise focused on today.

What are some of the happiest moments in my life?

For our final list (for the moment, anyway), I want you to cast your mind back over your life and find me ten moments when you can say you felt real joy – true happiness. They can be from any stage of life, so take your time with this one.

This time, I want you to try to not only think of the moment, but also record just what it was about that moment that led to your feeling of happiness. It may be an achievement you worked hard for or an important milestone, such as your wedding day or the birth of a child. Whatever the moment, try to record just what it was about it that made you happy.

To help you get started, an example might look like this:

Moment	What brought me joy
Wedding day	Everyone that really matters to me was in one place at one time.

So give it a go! This is one of those lists that you might want to spend some time on, but start somewhere.

Moment	What brought me joy

Your happiness themes

Finally, take a look at all four lists and look for some themes. If you had to put all of the entries into five main categories, what would they be? What is it that brings those moments together – is it a feeling? Is it the people or place? Try to work out what those happy moments have in common.

Examples of categories might be:

Family, friends, relationships

Social connection is what gives our lives meaning at the very core.

Passions

These are the fun things; you just love doing them and probably could do them all day (unfortunately, they are often not found in our jobs).

Purpose

This is what makes for a rich and fulfilling life. It is the sense of serving something bigger than you, the capacity to leave a legacy and the feeling that what you are doing matters.

Experiences

These create our memories, enabling us to explore, learn and grow.

If you have taken the time to work your way through these lists, there is a good chance you now have a great summary of some of the key moments and feelings you have experienced in your life.

It should come as no surprise that to cultivate more happiness in your life, you need to focus on creating more of those things in each day.

NO REGRETS

As I mentioned earlier, this morning I had a few moments sitting quietly in the sun with my aunt. She is one of my favourite people in the world. She and my uncle had a beautiful life together, full of the most amazing and unconventional adventures. Last year my uncle fell sick with cancer, and he passed away earlier this year. My aunt – his wife of almost fifty years – was and still is heartbroken. She is now a very fragile version of herself and it makes me so sad to see her this way. This morning, we spoke quietly of the beautiful moments in my uncle's life, his amazing achievements and his crazy adventures (for one, he drove a Kombi Van all the way from Australia to London in the 1960s, through countries we would never imagine entering today!).

Life is so short. Too short, I think. And it is not to be wasted. So why shouldn't we choose happiness? Why shouldn't we craft a life that we can love? We need a few downs to experience the ups.

But when it comes to happiness, for me, I often remind myself that my life is my life – the only one I will have. That it is important I lead my life true to myself – not by being selfish or causing harm to others, but by embracing every opportunity to live, as I was reminded to do this morning when talking with my aunt.

You may have heard of Bronnie Ware,[2] a palliative care nurse who has written about her experience and summarised her conversations with the dying. She identified her patients' top five regrets in life. They wished:

1. To have lived a life true to themselves and not the life that they thought was expected of them.

2. Not to have worked so hard and so much.

3. To have expressed their feelings more.

4. To have been better at keeping in touch with their friends.

5. To have let themselves be happier.

I remember reading Bronnie's blog post about this many years ago now; it struck a chord with me. Think about the possibility that we spend our lives working hard, striving for goals, aiming for success, but, along the way, miss the chance to enjoy what could truly make us happy. I think this outcome is more likely for we lawyers than for many other people I know. Our driven characters often mean we put our own needs to the side as we climb corporate ladders or aim for success. Bronnie's work really brought home for me the importance of living in the now, not working so much, focusing on the small things and, most importantly, allowing ourselves to be happier.

When all is said and done, we only get one chance at this. Surely, you want to give yourself the chance to enjoy every minute of whatever life wants

---

2   Bronnie Ware is author of The Top Five Regrets of the Dying – A Life Transformed by the Dearly Departing (http://bronnieware.com/regrets-of-the-dying/)

to throw at you. For me, family, friends, relationships, health, passions and purpose are the components of life that bring me happiness. And I expect I am not alone.

Being a lawyer is not really a part of this list for me. I can be happy without being a lawyer. But at the same time, being a lawyer delivers me the opportunity to find, experience and live so much happiness. Whether it be the people I meet, my friends and colleagues; the type of work I get to do, helping people at a time that is so difficult for them; or expressing my creativity, passions and purpose through writing, teaching and sharing – being a lawyer enables me to tap into and, on a daily basis, live the things that most matter to me. The things that, when they all come together, make me happy.

Law is the instrument that enables me to create the music that is my life. Being a lawyer may have a more or less significant part to play in your own happiness. We are all different, and the key here is to take the time to think about it – work out what makes you happy in your whole life, not just your work life.

I think, sometimes, we lawyers expect too much of our careers when it comes to our happiness. Work as a lawyer is hard – it is a profession where we spend our days getting people out of chaos, conflict and sometimes life-changing situations. We are a profession that's there to help, but, sadly, the people we help are rarely happy at the time we are working with them. We are often a part of them finding happiness again, but we rarely see the impact of our hard work.

It is important to keep things in perspective, to focus on your whole life in order to find the true meaning of happiness, not focus solely or too much on your work. You don't want to end your life regretting working too hard and too much, and not having allowed yourself to be happier.

FINDING MY HAPPINESS

I remember sitting at home on a Saturday night in November 2013. It was late and my husband and daughter were asleep (small miracles). I was sitting in our lounge surfing the internet, and I think I had recently watched the movie Julie and Julia – a beautiful film about a young American girl who has lost purpose and passion, and so decides to spend a year blogging her way through Julia Child's famous cookbook Mastering the Art of French Cooking. Now, let me be clear, I am no cook! But I had always loved the idea of a blog. And so, late that Saturday night for some completely unknown reason, I jumped on WordPress and set one up: 'The Happy Family Lawyer'.

And that was the moment I chose to be 'happy'.

The year 2013 was full of professional ups and downs. It was my daughter's second year of life and I was still working out what being a mum was all about, while regularly suffering from a severe lack of sleep. My office had been plagued with challenges and while my home life was great (if you ignore the sleepless nights), my work life was probably the worst it had ever been.

I decided to grab that unhappy bull by the horns and tell the world (and myself) that, from then on, I could and would find a way to ensure my happiness doing the work I do.

Because the thing is, I had (and have) so much to be happy about. It was just, at that time, I could not see it. The work I was doing, running a law firm and managing the people in it, was becoming a huge challenge. And I could not see a way out.

The point at which I started writing in 2013 was the point at which things changed – the moment in my 'lawyer life' where I found a renewed passion for what I was doing. Only a few months down the track, I started to feel happier.

I now know, looking back, that a huge part of me feeling happier came from the clarity of really considering just what it is that makes me happy – what happiness means to me. I wrote about it, shared it on my blog, devised happiness challenges, read a lot, and listened to and observed others with new vigour. I connected myself with people whom I considered happy and, in particular, found people who allowed me to feel happy.

I encourage you to do the same. You now have a list of moments, feelings, experiences and events in your life, organised into your happiness categories. Take those lists and carry them with you or put them on your office wall. Keep those reminders of what makes you happy with you and around you. Look for them each day, in every moment.

✳ ✳ ✳

Now we've looked at the meaning of happiness for you, we'll move on to consider the science behind the idea of being happy. We've broken down what happiness is on a practical level; now we'll delve into its mechanics. Just what is it that causes this feeling in our bodies, hearts and minds?

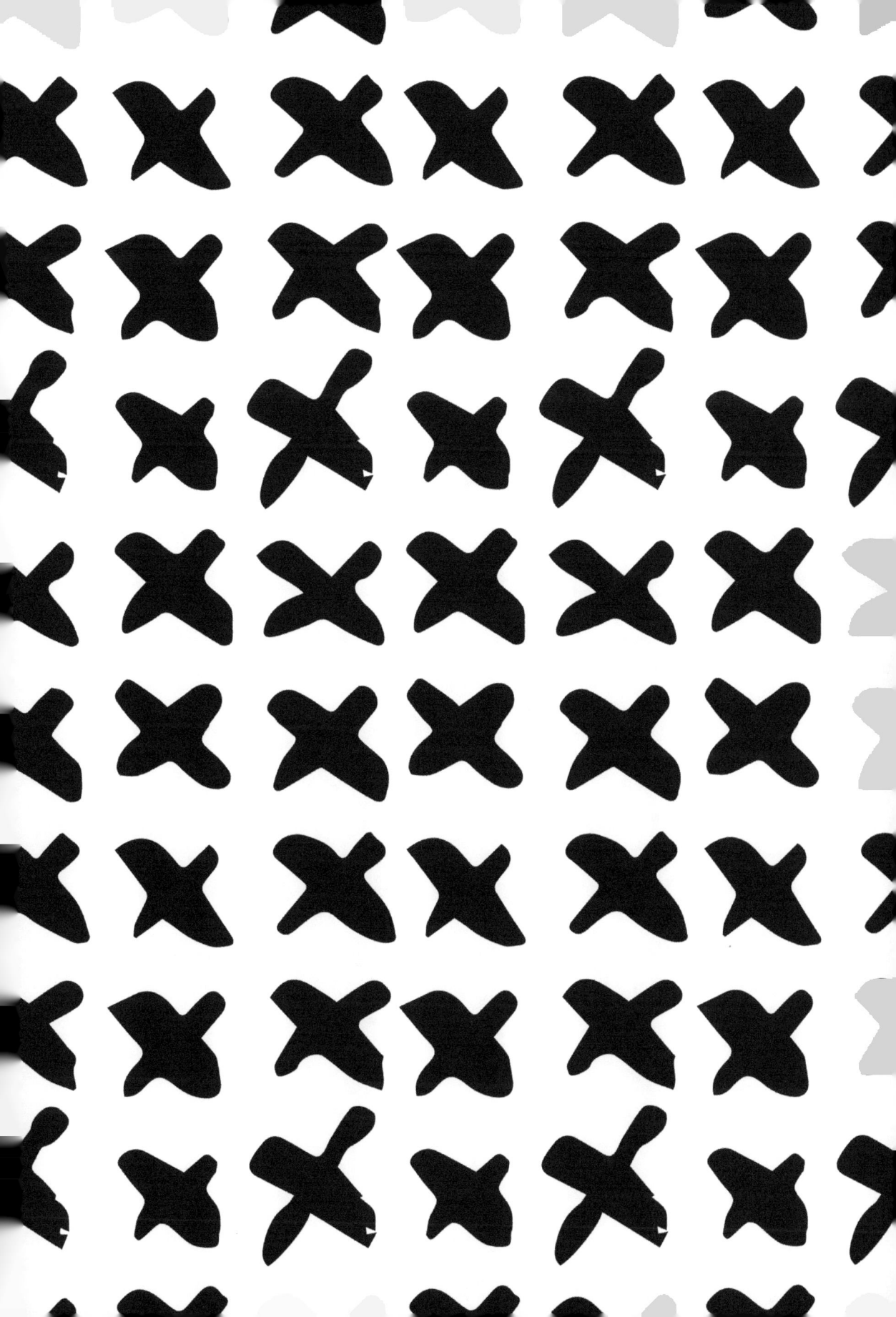

'What you think, you become. What you feel, you attract. What you imagine, you create.'

– BUDDHA –

The science of happiness

Being happy is a feeling. Measuring or assessing that feeling might seem impossible, but over the past decade, we have seen an explosion of science exploring happiness. This research is coming from two main areas:

Neuroscience

Through brain imaging and monitoring, neuroscientists have been able to explore the physical impact of happiness and other emotions on our brains and bodies. The new knowledge provides scientific answers when it comes to concepts many of us have just accepted or assumed to be true. For example, those of us who enjoy exercise just 'know' that it makes us feel better. The beauty of neuroscience is that we now have brain scans that show us why. This is a fast-developing area and makes for fascinating reading. Below, I have summarised some of the recent learnings, but there is a strong chance that by the time you read this, there will be even more depth to our understanding.

Psychology

There are two main fields of psychology in the study of happiness. The first is the realm of the evolutionary psychologists, who have considered the concept of happiness in the context of our evolution as a species. The second is the realm of the cognitive and social psychologists, often referred to as the positive psychologists, who use research and data collection to explore how our everyday lives, locations, careers and relationships affect our happiness levels. It is this area of positive psychology that I find most helpful when it comes to understanding happiness. Much of the psychology in this area focuses on how specific ways of thinking and acting affect our happiness. As you work through this book, you will come to see that much of what I have done and learned can be considered exploration of this area of science.

Though much that I share in this book is premised on the theories of positive psychology, I do think an understanding of the neuroscience is invaluable to better understanding why we feel the way we do from time to time, so let's take a closer look.

THE BASICS WHEN IT COMES TO OUR BRAIN AND HAPPINESS

To understand the neuroscience, we first need to understand a little about the biology and chemistry of our human brains. This is an area that you could read about for hours, and I would recommend it. I had the privilege of participating in a legal workshop last year that looked at neuroscience research and its application in law. It was fascinating and certainly taught me about the art of persuasion when it comes to our brains.

The human brain is something that scientists are only just starting to scratch the surface of in terms of understanding how it works. So far, we've come to know that, aside from being the command centre for most of our bodily systems and functions, it has a significant impact on our happiness.

Our brain consists of billions of nerve cells called neurons, which talk to each other via connections known as neural pathways. These pathways grow and change throughout our lives, depending on how we use our brains and our environment – this is called neuroplasticity.

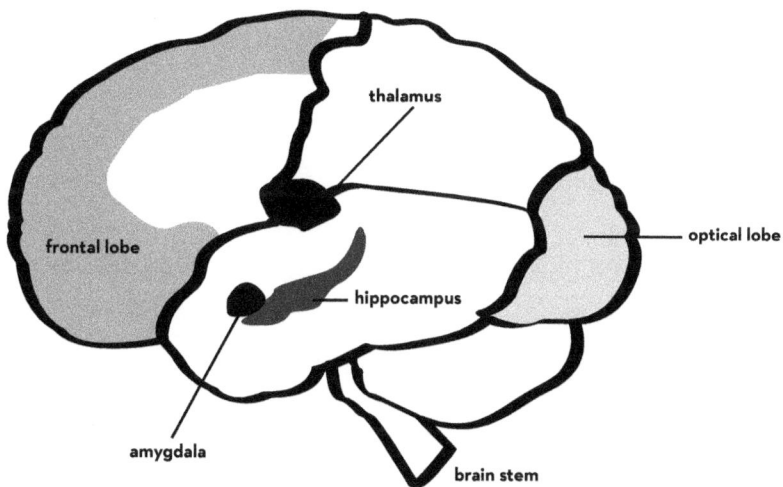

For the purpose of better understanding our happiness, it helps to understand the three key parts of our brain, their function and the role they play when it comes to our emotions. Each of these parts of our brain, although described separately, is innately interlinked. They do not operate independently, but rather have many interconnections through which the different parts influence each other.

The brain stem

This part of the brain is often referred to as our 'reptile brain' as it includes the main structures that are also found in the brain of a reptile – the brain stem and the cerebellum.

It was the first part of the brain to form and is in charge of the basics in terms of our body's functions – the control of our heart rate, breathing, sleeping, body temperature and eating. As such, it is not a part of the brain that I will talk about too much when it comes to happiness.

However, as this part of the brain is the conduit between our spinal cord and the more 'thinking' parts of our brain, it is responsible for sending messages that do affect our physical response to certain emotional events.

For example, you have probably heard the phrase 'fight or flight response'. The reptile brain is essential to triggering the physical response in the body's various systems to enable us to run fast or fight fast as necessary. I will talk much more about the 'higher level' parts of our brain, simply because they have a more direct correlation to our emotional state and our happiness; however, I think of the reptile brain as a processor of that emotion into the physical response – for example, the way our heartbeat races when we are scared.

The limbic system

This part of our brain is often referred to as the 'mammalian brain'. It was the second part to develop (100 million or so years ago!) and we share it with many other mammals. The limbic system is the emotional centre of the brain, hence its importance for our understanding of happiness. It is also involved in motivation, learning and memory.

There are two main parts of the limbic system that are particularly relevant to our discussion on happiness – the amygdala and the hippocampus.

The amygdala

The amygdala is a small, almond-shaped part of the brain that is responsible for fear, pleasure and empathy. As such, it plays a key role in our emotional lives.

While the amygdala does respond to positive sensation, it tends to have a much stronger response to negative situations. Once the amygdala takes hold and tells us we are 'scared', there is little chance of rational thought in any short amount of time. Daniel Goleman, author of the 1996 book Emotional Intelligence: Why It Can Matter More Than IQ, coined the phrase 'amygdala hijack' to describe the overwhelming emotional response we sometimes have when the amygdala feels threatened.

As a divorce lawyer, I talk a lot about amygdala hijack, as I see it in my clients regularly. Most of us have had our hearts broken at one time or another, so you probably know that heartbreak brings a terrible wave of emotion that seems impossible to control. This is a great example of amygdala hijack – when we are in this deep emotional state, our capacity to make decisions and process information becomes very, very limited because our brain literally stops us from being able to take that information and send it to our neocortex, where complex, rational thinking and logic takes place.

You know you are facing amygdala hijack when you feel a strong emotional reaction that comes on really quickly and, when you look back later, you think to yourself that your reaction or behaviour may have been 'over the top' or disproportionate to the stressor.

We have all experienced amygdala hijack at some stage. In the work setting, you might recall colleagues who exploded in response to a menial challenge. Sometimes, we describe this colloquially as the 'straw that broke the camel's back'. We can manage and control our stress and emotions for only so long before something happens that on any other day might mean nothing, but today tips you right over. That is your amygdala moving into a fear response, and there is no coming back quickly.

Simply put, when the amygdala is sending out 'be very scared' messages, we cannot be happy.

The good news is that we can train our brain to identify when an amygdala hijack is imminent. The work of Daniel Goleman on emotional intelligence in the workplace, particularly among leaders, is very powerful. Goleman describes emotional intelligence as our ability to understand, identify and manage our own emotions and those of others around us.

Like all research, Goleman's has been criticised, but his theories have been widely adopted in the business and leadership communities. And to me, it makes a lot of sense – the more calm, considered and self-aware we can be, the better decisions we will be able to make, and those traits will rub off on those around us as well.

Amygdala hijack is pretty commonplace for lawyers, and even more commonplace for our clients. The cost of this can be huge – in the workplace, this sort of response will often be associated with poor behaviour and explosive outbursts of anger. Clearly, these traits do not make for a great place to work. They create stress for the person having the response and stress for those around them, too. Emotions are contagious and these responses create unhappiness that spreads.

In our clients, we see the same emotional reactions to the stressors that have brought them into our offices in the first place. For me, it is divorce. My clients are going through one of the most significant grief events they may ever experience. They are under significant stress and, as such, it doesn't take much for their amygdala to be hijacked. Our capacity to assist our clients when they are in these deep, emotionally reactive states is very limited. But there are some tools we can use to benefit them and us:

- **Take a 'time out'** – Stop what you are doing. If you can break the immediate response by removing yourself from the trigger, you can keep the logic and reason part of your brain engaged.

- **Breathe** – If you feel the fear response coming or taking over, concentrate on your breath. Breathe slowly and with purpose, and focus only on the movement in your body – this will also help to keep your neocortex engaged.

- **Be present** – When you are actively present in any situation, you have your neocortex engaged. If you can be actively present, with purpose and without judgment, there is a good chance the amygdala will not be triggered. Some days we are great at this, and other days we are not so great, but if you can start by trying to keep your mind focused on one task at a time, and look at the world from a place of curiosity rather than judgment, you will find managing your own emotional responses and the responses of those around you to be far more achievable.

With my clients, I have found that merely opening a dialogue from a very early stage about the impact of grief on their brains, and normalising their emotions, has assisted in reducing the chance of amygdala hijack or extreme responses.

The hippocampus

Also part of the limbic system, the hippocampus is largely responsible for memory and learning. The hippocampus processes our new memories for storage in our long-term memory and is the part of the brain largely responsible for memory recall. In Alzheimer's patients, the hippocampus is one of the first areas of the brain to be damaged, leading to memory loss and disorientation. The hippocampus is covered with receptors for the stress hormone cortisol – this part of our brain can be damaged if we are exposed to significant or long-term stress. The cortisol literally eats away at this part of our brain, reducing its size and functionality. Damage to the hippocampus means damage to our memory pathways, meaning we are less able to form new memories.[3]

It is possible to train and develop this part of our brain. A great example of this involves a study of the brains of London taxi drivers. Researchers from the McGill University in Montreal, Canada, compared the size of the hippocampus of these drivers to people who did not have to drive taxis and found that this part of the brain was measurably larger in the drivers. To be a London taxi driver, you have to memorise and quickly recall a vast number of interwoven street maps and suburbs, requiring extensive visual-spatial memory.[4]

So for we lawyers who have to retain and recall bundles of legislation, case law, facts and cases (which probably look a lot like the London road system to our brains), it clearly helps to have a hippocampus that is working really well. This also generally makes for a happier lawyer who can more easily recall the information they need to be great at their job.

---

3   Research reported by the Greater Good Science Center at Berkley University
4   Research reported at http://www.pnas.org/content/97/8/4398.full

There are ways we can 'grow' our hippocampus to give us the best chance of maximising its function and, in turn, our memory and learning. Some researchers have associated regular exercise and being physically fit with having a bigger hippocampus. A study I found during my research compared two different groups of mice. One group exercised on a mouse wheel each day, while another group had no access to a wheel and were found to have a much smaller hippocampus.[5] (You will start to see a recurring theme soon – regular exercise is the solution for so many things!). Eating a diet high in omega-3 fatty acids and nuts has also been found to help us grow our hippocampus. [6]

Of course, to avoid 'shrinking' our hippocampus, we need to limit our exposure to long-term stress, anxiety or untreated depression. And while regular exercise is said to help us increase the size of our hippocampus, a lack of exercise and poor diet is being shown to shrink this part of our brain.[7]

Are you seeing the theme? Eat well and exercise, and your brain (well, parts of it anyway) will get bigger, work better and hopefully keep working for longer.

The cortex

This is the outer part of our brain and is often referred to as the 'new mammalian brain'. The cortex emerged with the primates, but it is our prefrontal cortex – the part of our brain that sits right behind our forehead – that sets us apart from the rest of our primate friends.

---

[5]   To learn more, consider this article by Dr Majid Fotuhi, Neuroscientist: http://sharpbrains.com/blog/2015/11/04/can-you-grow-your-hippocampus-yes-heres-how-and-why-it-matters/

[6]   See the article above from Dr Majid Fotuhi, Neuroscientist

[7]   See the article above from Dr Majid Fotuhi, Neuroscientist

It is this part of our brain that enables us to move past the emotional functions of the limbic system and into a space of reasoned, rational and logical thought.

The prefrontal cortex is where emotion is processed. It interacts with the limbic system, particularly the amygdala, to process and understand our emotions.

In researching this book, I fell upon an article that referenced the work of Joseph LeDoux, a neuroscientist at the Center for Neural Science at New York University.[8] In his work, LeDoux has considered the relationship between our 'thinking/logic brain', the neocortex (of which the prefrontal cortex is a part), and the dangerous (but fun) amygdala we discussed earlier. He has pinpointed the neural pathways bringing information to the brain through the senses, and discovered that information entering through the eyes or ears goes first to the thalamus, which acts as a sort of mail sorter by deciding which parts of the brain to send the information to.

When the information coming in is emotional, the thalamus sends out two signals – the first to the amygdala and the second to the neocortex. This means that the amygdala has the information first and can react quickly, before our thinking brain has even received the information and considered the options. This is amygdala hijack in action!

If there is a part of the brain that is important for us lawyers, the prefrontal cortex, or thinking brain, really has to be it. The two halves of the prefrontal cortex also seem to have specialised functions – the left is more involved in establishing positive feelings, while the right is in charge of negative feelings.

Psychologist Dr Richard Davidson, who established the Center for Healthy Minds at the University of Wisconsin-Madison,[9] has studied in depth the biochemical reactions that occur between our limbic system and

---

8   To learn more about the work of Joseph LeDoux, visit: http://www.cns.nyu.edu/corefaculty/LeDoux.php
9   http://centerhealthyminds.org/about/founder-richard-davidson

the frontal lobes. Dr Davidson states that our frontal lobes are involved in both thought and emotion. It is perhaps no surprise, then, that our thinking affects the way we feel and the way we feel affects our thinking (we now have the brain scans and research that prove it!). This is really where the area of positive psychology comes in and I will talk about it more shortly but, simply put, psychologists like Dr Davidson focus on how we can intentionally use our thoughts to change our emotion.

So here is the thing. When I decided almost three years ago to choose to be happy, I was altering my thoughts and activating my thinking brain, which, in turn, affected my limbic system and the way I feel (in a great way).

Through his research, Dr Davidson has shown that the left side of our frontal lobe is more active when we feel happy. The right side is more active when we feel sad. And so, if we focus on what stimulates the left side of our prefrontal cortex, we can start to train ourselves to feel happier. The reverse is true as well – by better understanding what calms the right side of our prefrontal cortex, we can train our brains to better manage sadness.

Davidson has found that mindful meditation has the effect of strengthening the left side of our frontal lobe (the happiness centre) while at the same time calming the right side. And the really good news is that having fun, hanging out with people you love, doing things you love and pursuing your purpose and meaning will all help to stimulate your left prefrontal cortex.

The Center for Healthy Minds is doing a lot of work in the area of neuroplasticity – researching the capacity for our brains to be 'sculpted', or retrained and re-organised, by creating new neural pathways to promote healthy habits, including wellness and happiness. Research is showing that our brain can be trained at all stages of life. And anyone who has decided to learn a new hobby, language or career later in life can attest to this.

As Dr Davidson says, 'The invitation in all of this work is that we can take more responsibility for our own brains and shape our brains wittingly in a more intentional way by cultivating healthy habits of mind.' [10]

The news is good if you are looking for a happier state of being. Once you come to understand just how your brain is wired, you can start to change things. You can calm those emotional and stress responses, and increase activity in your happiness centre.

DON'T FORGET THOSE HAPPINESS HORMONES

Now that you have an understanding of brain structure and function, we can't leave a discussion about our brains without touching on the five major chemicals that influence our happiness:

Dopamine

We often hear of dopamine being the 'happiness-inducing drug', but that is not really the case. Dopamine is nature's reward for searching for food or sex – the essentials for survival and reproduction. It is not really a chemical source of happiness; it's more about survival. This neurotransmitter does a number of things in our bodies. It is best known for flowing through our brains when we anticipate something pleasurable is about to happen.

---

10   http://centerhealthyminds.org/join-the-movement/the-science-of-a-happy-mind

Dopamine is associated with reward-seeking behaviour, as it helps us both see the reward and achieve it. Set a goal and achieve it and you will be rewarded with little hits of dopamine.

For some lawyers, these dopamine hits can be hard to come by during work hours, which is not always a bad thing. However, by bringing new experiences into your working week, you can help pump a little extra dopamine into your brain, and come a step closer to happiness.

Serotonin

This is commonly known as the main chemical responsible for mood balance. Serotonin is also linked to feeling good and living longer (both of which I am very interested in!). Low levels of serotonin have been associated with conditions such as depression. The good news is that we can naturally increase our body's production of serotonin through exercise, a healthy diet, exposure to daylight and other fun stuff. So take your lunch outside today, lie on your back and dream a bit of a happy dream – hopefully those serotonin levels will start to soar.

Oxytocin

The hugging hormone! Oxytocin is a key part of our need and desire to form meaningful relationships with others. There is no end of research into the impact and effects of oxytocin, and some of the more recent research I have seen suggests links between oxytocin and our capacity to feel trust and empathy towards others.[11]

---

11   PhD work of Dr C. Sue Carter of the University of Illinois: https://kiweb.iu.edu/about/profiles/cscarter.php

Relationships, intimacy, love, empathy and trust all add to our sense of happiness, so perhaps it is time to give and get some hugs for a bit of an oxytocin boost today. If you are not really the hugging type, then gift-giving has also been said to assist with the production of oxytocin, so perhaps try that instead.

Endorphins

We love endorphins! They are released to help alleviate stress, anxiety and pain, and apparently have an effect on our bodies similar to that of morphine. They are best known for being increased after a good round of exercise. You might have heard of a 'runner's high' – anyone who is a great lover of exercise, particularly running, will attest to the great feeling you get after the event (the problem is the bit where you have to convince yourself to start the run in the first place!).

Aside from regular exercise, one of the easiest ways to increase endorphins is to laugh. So take time for some jokes – bad or otherwise – to get a bit of laughter into your day.

Cortisol

In the most simplistic sense, cortisol is a stress chemical. We don't want too much cortisol in our brain, as that tends to mean we are moving into our limbic centre and bordering on a 'flight, fight or freeze' response to a situation. This is fine if you have the occasional fight with a tiger or lion, after which your cortisol level goes back to normal. But for many of us, the stresses of modern life mean that our body thinks we are in an eternal fight with that tiger and so produces high levels of cortisol for too long. However, having some cortisol in our system is healthy, giving us the capacity to manage the good and the bad, and those stressful moments.

Too little cortisol can leave us feeling chronically tired. The good news is that a wholesome diet, regular exercise and meditation are all known to regulate cortisol levels in our bodies.

POSITIVE PSYCHOLOGY

I have touched already on some of the important concepts of positive psychology when it comes to our brain function and, of course, our happiness. The work of Dr Richard Davidson at the Center for Healthy Minds is among the easiest to read and understand.

Simply put, at the heart of positive psychology lies the idea that we can intentionally use our thoughts to change our feelings in a positive way. It is this aspect of the science of happiness that I have focused on in my own life.

That moment in 2013 when I said to myself, 'I choose to be happy,' was the beginning of my shift into this world of positive psychology. I had no idea at the time, but that act of intentionally choosing to seek happiness was the simple beginning of a significant change in my own happiness.

I could talk about the various theories of the psychology of happiness for pages and pages, but I want to come back to the simple idea at the core of this area of psychology – that we can use our thoughts to change our feelings.

The idea that how we think, what we do and how we spend our time will have a significant impact on our happiness seems sensible to me. When it comes to our brain structure and function, there are things that may be out of our control, but we can intentionally change our thoughts, what we do each day and how we spend our time. It is this science that I will focus on in the balance of this book.

NEUROSCIENCE AND POSITIVE PSYCHOLOGY FOR HAPPINESS 101

Here are a few great places to go for more up-to-date reading and resources:

1.   **Center for Healthy Minds –**
centerhealthyminds.org

2.   **Greater Good Science Center, University of Berkeley –**
greatergood.berkeley.edu/

3.   **The Happiness Institute, Australia –**
www.thehappinessinstitute.com

* * *

Once we understand, even at a basic level, the science of what is happening inside our bodies, we can start to design our daily life to activate our positive chemicals and train our brain to better respond to difficult situations. So begins the creation of the happy lawyer.

*

The next part of the book addresses how to do this in practice, cultivating the five drivers of happiness in law and, more importantly, in life.

PART TWO:

The HAPPY

Lawyer

Some days are sunny, and other days are stormy.

- JENNIFER DULSKI -

Choose happiness

It has taken me two-and-a-half years of active, mindful thoughts and behaviours to find myself in a place where I can safely say to you that I am happy. I am a happy lawyer both at work and, more importantly, out of my office – with my family, friends and the world at large. This is not to say that I don't ever experience unhappiness any more. But I think the difference for me, now, is that I have tools I can use that help me to refocus, to find the positives, to put things in perspective and to be happy again, sooner. I spend more of my time being happy now than ever before. And I truly believe that this is because I choose happiness.

Instead of seeing all the problems, the things I dislike and the stuff that is not going well, I choose to look for the good, the little wins and the things that are going well. I practise gratitude every day. I focus on leading my life with kindness and curiosity, rather than judgment. And I focus on slowing down, on being mindful, living in the moment, and enjoying life for what it is. I have taken ownership of my own story, my own life, and have made a positive and active choice to seek happiness. And it has worked.

I have watched a few of my closest friends struggle their way through their careers in law. From the outside, they are the epitome of success, but I have seen them suffer on the inside from a deep unhappiness rooted in the fact that the profession at which they are so talented is affecting their lives in such a negative way. I observed first-hand a talented law graduate being worked into the ground and leaving law, all within the first eighteen months of her career. And she's not the only one. It is these stories that really worry me because it seems they are not unique to my friendship circle – these are issues that are being discussed and debated in almost every legal publication and at every legal conference nationwide. Then, if we look beyond Australia, the same issues seem to be arising in the United Kingdom, Canada and America. In short, lawyers the western world over are unhappy, disillusioned and leaving the profession in large numbers.

I am all for everyone following their own path, choosing their own life and finding happiness, but I really do hope we can find a way to keep both our up-and-coming, and established, great lawyers in law. I like to think that part of the secret to this is opening a dialogue about what it takes to be happy in law, and opening a dialogue for change – change that will educate lawyers about the drivers of happiness and, moreover, their ability to choose a happy life.

My experience of happiness in law has really come for me in the past two or so years, as a result of educating myself and making that choice. But what are you actually choosing to change? What is the magic answer to the question:

'How do you find happiness?'

THE FIVE DRIVERS OF HAPPINESS IN LAW (AND IN LIFE!)

There were a few themes that kept coming up when I addressed what it would take to experience happiness, not only as a lawyer, but also as someone engaged in life in general. When I sat down and really looked at what everyone was saying, those themes could be put into five broad categories:

Good health

When we are in poor health, we are unhappy. We feel terrible, we can't operate at our peak and everything is just harder. We lawyers are notorious for neglecting our health, engaging in a lifestyle that embraces overworking, poor eating, not exercising and, of course, drinking away our worries with alcohol.

Those lawyers around me whom I consider to be happy are all healthy. While some of them may be able to regularly run marathons, most of them just look after themselves by eating well, exercising regularly and spending time calming their mind to ensure they are in the best state they can be.

A positive attitude

Our attitude, or our mindset, is essential to our happiness (as the neuroscience we discussed earlier explains). Our capacity to be positive, grateful and live in the moment, as well as our ability to focus on what is great in life, accept challenges and rise above them will have a significant impact on our day-to-day experience of happiness.

A burning passion

Happy lawyers are passionate! They not only find the time to pursue their dreams outside of work, but have also found a way to work those passions into their everyday routine.

A defining purpose

Living with purpose is essential to our happiness. Purpose is what makes for a rich and fulfilling life. It is the sense of being part of something bigger than you, knowing that what you do matters, and having the capacity to leave a legacy.

A sense of self

You need to be comfortable with who you are in the world, proud to be that person at work, at home and in all aspects of your life. Being authentically you is the final key to being a happy lawyer.

Almost every lawyer I have interviewed has found that their own happiness meant finding a way to work each of these five elements into their daily life, particularly into their practice of law.

✷ ✷ ✷

To make things simple, I have taken those themes and summarised them in a way that's easy to remember … find me a lawyer who doesn't like a checklist!

✓ *Health*

✓ *Attitude*

✓ *Passion*

✓ *Purpose*

✓ *You*

Now we're going to look at each of these aspects in turn, along with guidance and practical exercises that will help you 'tick them off' and create a real difference in your life.

'Happiness is
good health
and a
bad memory'

– INGRID BERGMAN –

H is for Health

When it comes to happiness, good health is absolutely essential. Without good health, we really cannot do anything. When I refer to 'health', I am referring to physical health, mental health and our overall wellness.

If you are not looking after yourself and making your health and wellness your top priority, you will struggle with stress. I expect you feel tired and run down most of the time and suffer from illnesses, such as colds and flus, with some regularity. For me, any discussion about health and wellness begins with fuel, proceeds quickly to movement and ends with rest.

HOW ARE YOU FUELLING YOUR TANK?

Let's imagine you are a car. Not a fancy one, just a standard Mazda that requires unleaded petrol to run. But you decide to fill the tank with diesel.

No real reason why; it just seems easier, quicker and cheaper. In fact, you don't really even think about it – you just fill up the tank and don't really check the type of petrol.

What will happen to your Mazda? Well, I am no mechanic, but I expect it won't take long before your car stops functioning. It simply won't start. And, perhaps more importantly, the damage you have done to the fuel lines won't be apparent when you look at the car from the outside, but will soon become obvious when your trusty mechanic pops the bonnet and has a good look inside. The engine will be ruined and you will have a very, very expensive problem to fix.

Our bodies are the same. Food and fluid are our fuel, and if you fill your body with cheap, processed diesel when it was designed to have fresh, wholesome food and water, it shouldn't be a surprise when your engine starts breaking down.

We all know we need to eat a well-balanced diet! In my experience, the issue for lawyers is not that they don't want to, but that finding the time in a busy day to eat well is pushed down the list of priorities. When you make it to work, you grab your coffee, your head is down working and, before you know it, it's 3pm. Then 7pm, and it is a mad scramble to find dinner quick because you're starving. It is at this point that food from the takeaway next door to your office looks so delightfully appetising.

Most lawyers I know don't go out of their way to eat unhealthily; they just don't seem to put fuel high enough on their list of things to worry about during the day to ensure that the right fuel is purchased.

Food = fuel = performance

Being a lawyer is a 'mind job'. To do our best, we need our brains working at optimum performance levels all the time. If we were cars, I like to think we would be a luxury model – Porsche, Rolls Royce, Bentley or perhaps even Tesla. If you own a Porsche, I expect you don't fill it with the cheapest unleaded fuel. I imagine if I owned one, I would fill it with some sort of fancy, high-performance fuel that would make it purr.

It all started for me with this mind shift. As a woman, I have spent most of my life associating food and what I eat with the word 'diet'. I have always eaten well, but I was more worried about how I looked than how I felt.

Thanks to social media, modern life and just general information overload, we are constantly surrounded with information about diet, food, health – what we should eat, what we shouldn't, the latest 'superfood' and, of course, the latest weight-loss fad.

This past year, I have changed my outlook on food. Now what I eat is all about ensuring that I am keeping my body, and more importantly, my brain, fuelled, so that I can perform at the best of my physical ability. I can't believe it took me forty years to have this epiphany!

By simply changing how I think about food and eating better as a result, I have found the mental capacity to manage difficult situations, stress and challenge, and my ability to think clearly, even when things are hard, has significantly improved.

Eating to improve your brain

Research across the world is looking into the impact of diet on our physical and mental health, and the capacity of our bodies to develop and function.

What's intriguing about much of the research is that there are clear connections being formed between the types of food we eat and our susceptibility to mental health conditions such as depression.

For example, in countries where the diet is very high in fish and other Omega-3 rich foods, such as Japan, it has been noted that depression levels are very low. Omega-3 fatty acids include DHA, which has been found to be very important in terms of the functioning of the neurons in our brains. Dr Samir Samman, an Associate Professor in Human Nutrition at the University of Sydney, notes that the human brain is comprised of nearly sixty per cent fat, much of which is Omega-3 fat or DHA. DHA is a building block in our brains and is also used to make and replenish neurotransmitters, which transfer messages between different parts of our brain. Research consistently shows that there is a strong link between Omega-3 intake and good brain health, including lower rates of depression and suicide in adults. Oily fish is one of the best sources of DHA, so make sure you have some salmon and tuna in your diet regularly.

When it comes to memory, a 2007 study published in the American Journal of Clinical Nutrition found that women with sufficient iron levels were able to perform much faster in mental tests than women who were iron deficient. Iron is essential for producing dopamine and noradrenaline in our brain, as well as for carrying oxygen to our brains. Low levels of iron, therefore, affect our concentration and memory. Unfortunately, iron is one of the most common nutrient deficiencies in the developed world.

Iron-rich foods include red meat, fish, poultry, green vegetables such as spinach, silverbeet and broccoli, lentils and beans, and nuts and seeds.

Substances that can help our memory include:

- **Foods high in Vitamin E -** These include healthy vegetable oil, seeds and nuts, peanut butter and wholegrains, all of which have been said to help the neurons or nerve cells in our brains. In Alzheimer's disease, neurons in certain parts of the brain start to die. In terms of retaining memory, eating these foods may safeguard these neurons.

- **Folate/Vitamin B9** - Folate, which is found in fruit and vegetables, has also been found to help prevent memory loss. By eating broccoli, bran cereals, asparagus, and berries such as strawberries and blueberries, we can add a folate boost to our diet.

- **Glucose** - Our brains need glucose in large amounts to function properly. Glucose comes from carbohydrates but, unlike our muscles, our brain cannot store it, which means we need to keep it constantly filled. Eating regular meals and small snacks with a combination of proteins and carbohydrates goes a long way to keeping the glucose levels in your brain constant.

- **Vitamin C** - Researchers at the University of Sydney have found that there is a link between sufficient levels of Vitamin C and an increase in memory and function. Foods that are high in Vitamin C include citrus fruits, tomatoes, broccoli, capsicum and berries.

Eating to improve our brain is important for us as lawyers, as we need strong memory recall and the capacity to focus. We know that we are at significant risk of depression, so anything we can do in terms of dietary change to increase our brain function and, at the same time, minimise the risk of mental health conditions makes sense.

Finding the time

When it comes to eating well, there is a plethora of information available on what this really means. And I think most of us know the basics:

1.   Fresh food.

2.   Balanced diet – a bit from each of the five food groups we learned about at school (fruit, vegetables, meat and fish, grains, dairy).

3.   Regular meals and snacks (and this does include breakfast!).

4.   Lots and lots and lots of water.

5.   Avoiding processed, manufactured, fast foods and sugary foods (sadly, most of the stuff we love to eat for comfort falls in this category).

When it comes to what we eat, one of the biggest challenges I came across when chatting with my lawyer friends was a lack of time. Most of them knew they needed to eat well and had a great understanding of what that meant; the problem was there was no time to fit it in.
You have to make time.

Health is my 'Number 1 Happiness Attribute' for a good reason – without our health, nothing else really matters. I want to live for as long as I can and, simply put, to give myself the best chance of achieving this, I need to be as healthy as I can be. This starts with eating really well.

I run a business (well, three businesses, really), organise a team of over ten, and have a husband and a daughter. Like you, I am busy, and time is precious to me. So I have to make my fuel a top priority to ensure that I give myself the best chance of being healthy.

Below are a few tips to help you do the same, which really come down to one big timesaver – planning ahead!

In our house, my husband and I both work full time (I am really lucky he does all the cooking during the week – thank you, Ollie!). We realised earlier this year that cooking and eating dinner had become such a chore. We were eating the same stuff all the time. It was good food, but getting out and organising stuff each day for dinner was a pain, and we just didn't have the time, so, inevitably, three or so nights a week, takeaway seemed like a better idea.

This year, I found Aussie Farmers Direct. There are lots of these businesses to choose from, and it has been a great game-changer for our family. Each Monday, a big box of fruit, vegetables and meat is dropped to my office. In that box are the ingredients for our dinners for the week – recipes and all. We have no idea what is coming, but it is all fresh, yummy and the meals take only a few minutes to cook (it is so easy even I cook occasionally!).

We don't mind cooking (in fact, I think Ollie secretly loves it) – our issue was the 'brain time' needed to think about what to cook and getting the ingredients to do it. This one decision to sign up and have all we need for the week of meals arrive on a Monday has saved us at least three hours a week and probably $100 or more as well.

Have a think about where you are spending your time when it comes to your meals – thanks to this wonderful thing called the internet, you could set up a recurring online shopping order, use a service like Aussie Farmers or even do a big Sunday bake-up and freeze meals and lunches for the week. Have a think about just what your barrier is to eating well and see if you can't find a better way around the problem. (You're a lawyer, remember? Problem-solving is your thing.)

Planning ahead is also possible in the office. I used to find myself each day getting to work not having had breakfast, realising it was almost 2pm and the local lunch shops were closing, and then missing dinner because I was out at a meeting. I would fall into bed having hardly eaten a thing all day.

It may have taken me almost twenty years in this job but I have finally learned to plan ahead. My big secret here – smoothies are your new best friend! The smoothie craze has taken the world by storm. I was a little slow to get on that wave and ride it, but now I have, my mornings have changed for the better. If you are like me and getting in breakfast is near impossible, then embrace the smoothie!

Now, when I say smoothie, I don't mean chocolate milkshake. Take the recipe I have for a cacao, banana, hazelnut and almond milk smoothie, for example, which tastes better than any chocolate milkshake I have ever had. This is now my staple breakfast treat on days where I know things are going to be hard.

Buy a blender, visit the back of this book for some great smoothie recipes (and more!) and get onto it. Your breakfast smoothie will easily get you through to mid-morning and feed the kids as well.

The next part of my planning meant that I organised a weekly delivery of fruit to our office so that I (and everyone working with me) had a big bowl of healthy snacks to grab all week. Then I stacked my office fridge with yoghurt, berries and bananas, so even if I couldn't get out for lunch, I had a back-up plan ready to roll.

The days when I was out of my office, in Court, teaching or in mediation, were always the hardest when it came to finding the time to eat well. Now, planning ahead, I take lots of snacks with me (healthy ones!). I have my smoothie on the way and I don't leave home without a bottle of water, which I keep refilling all day.

This may all sound so simple, but the message is important – put your health first so you can live your best life. What you eat is a huge part of that.

YOU HAVE TO MOVE!

We can't talk about being healthy without talking about the need to move. We have to exercise! Our bodies are designed to move, to be agile, to run around.

As lawyers, we get to sit at a desk, hunched over, often for hours at a time. And we are busy. We don't really have time to move, to exercise, to go to the gym, so we don't. This means, of course, that we put on weight, become less healthy, eat more poorly and, well ... you know where this all goes.

I love to exercise. It makes me feel great. I grew up doing lots of sport, dancing, swimming, running, always something, but even I, with such a love of exercise, have found it really hard to keep movement in my daily lawyer life. Once I had my daughter, it got really, really hard.

But here is the thing, when we exercise, our bodies produce a whole array of great chemicals that have the added bonus of making us feel happy. So, when it comes to movement, I encourage you to have another mindset shift. Declare, 'Exercise is my new happiness drug, and I will swallow it every day!'

Why should lawyers exercise?

Our bodies developed thousands of years ago, when we were spending our days moving around almost all the time. Modern life has, of course, meant a shift to a more sedentary life for most of us. And the life of a lawyer, unless you happen to be a criminal lawyer running between bail courts on a Monday, involves sitting at a desk with a computer most of the time.

Without exercise, no matter how healthy your diet, there is a good chance you will lose muscle tone, bone strength and general body function. If we aim to live for as long as we can and be in the best shape along the way, we need strong bones, muscles and brains, so this is where our need to exercise kicks in.

The benefits of exercise are numerous. Perhaps the most obvious is that exercise boosts endorphins in our body – the chemicals we spoke about earlier which act as happy juice for our brains. Endorphins alleviate stress, anxiety and pain, so why wouldn't you make sure you get a hit of endorphins every day?

Research has shown over and over again that when your lifestyle includes regular exercise (and I mean more than walking to the photocopier four times a day), you will:

- Be better able to manage stress.

- Be healthier – likely carrying less weight and having lower susceptibility to illness.

- Be more energetic, which means being more productive both at work and outside of work.

- Be in a better mood.

- Be able to sleep better.

- Be in possession of better memory and boosted intelligence.

- Be at lower risk of dementia in old age.

Looking at that list, why wouldn't you add exercise to your daily routine?

Finding the time

The one thing we all have in common is the number of hours, minutes and seconds in a day. We all have exactly the same amount of time. So pause for a moment. When you say to yourself, 'I just don't have enough time,' what you are really saying is, 'I have more important things to do with my time.'

Do you really have more important things to do with your time than look after your own health? Could there possibly be a more important thing in your life?

Your job this week is to find the time every day to move with energy – to exercise for at least half an hour. I don't necessarily want you to join a gym (though do, by all means, if you really want to). I just want you to move.

If you are in need of some ideas, here is my seven-day movement challenge. Are you ready for some fun?

Day 1

Just to be clear, by Day 1, I mean today, not another day when you feel ready to fit this in. Find your ten favourite dance tracks. Put them in a playlist. Load up your music dock and run on the spot, dance, skip, spin a hoola hoop, run around the house, jump on the kids' trampoline or sprint up and down your office until all those ten songs have played. Each song should be about three to four minutes, and if you really need to, you can do one song at a time, but your job is to make it through all ten. TODAY! (If you happen to be reading this at ten o'clock at night, you can start tomorrow, but otherwise you have no excuse and must start today.)

Once you are done, I want you to grab a piece of paper and a pen and write down three words that describe how you feel.

Day 2

Today you are going for a walk. A fast walk, not a casual stroll – the sort of walk where you feel puffed (imagine those Olympic walkers with that funny hip shuffle – that is you today!). Take your playlist with you if you like and walk until it is done. If you are at work and there is 'no time', you are going to have to find the time, so consider a walking meeting with that colleague you need to chat to anyway (just make sure you remind them to bring their sneakers too), or grab your phone and dictate that letter as you go if you have to. I really encourage you to stop all work for thirty minutes, step out of your office or your home and walk fast. Take in the beautiful surrounds. Try to be in the moment and turn your brain off, just for a few moments.

When you are back, pull out that piece of paper and write down three words that describe how you feel again.

Day 3

Today is the day for the 'dictatathon'! Now, if you are an old school lawyer like me who loves a dictaphone, this one is for you! If you are not, that's okay – you will just have to swap it for your phone. Your challenge today is to stand every time you pick up that dictaphone or phone. While you are standing, dictaphone in hand, you are going to march on the spot, bend your knees, or try and touch your toes if you can (you may need to be creative with the dictaphone-holding for that one!). Do some squats, stretch your back and if you are a yoga guru, take a call while balancing on one leg.

Do this all day and at the end of the day, write down three words that describe how you feel.

Day 4

Today is race day. If you are at home, set that oven timer to thirty minutes and if you are at work, set your phone alarm. In the next thirty minutes (you can do two fifteen-minute slots if you have to), your task is to run around as fast as you can to clean your home or your office. If you have a cubicle, not an office, either feel free to extend your cleaning to the office kitchen or leave it for home in the evening. Grab that vacuum and clean up in a frenzy. Turn up the playlist again and dance around as you dust and mop. If the kids and your partner are home, get them involved too. This should be crazy, fun and fast. All the while, your job is to move!

When you are done, write down those three words again.

Day 5

Today we are going on a walkathon. Hopefully, it is a work day and, better still, you work in a firm where billable units are king. Set the alarm on your phone to go off once every hour today. When it does, take a six-minute unit to walk around your office, down the fire stairs, outside and around the block. You can walk on the spot if it helps, but wherever you are, you need to walk once an hour for one billable unit, six times today. Between each unit walk, see if you can turn off your email and phone and just focus on one task for the remaining nine units of that hour. See how much you can get done when the distractions are turned off before it is time to go for a walk again.

At the end of the day, give me three words that describe how you feel.

Day 6

We are almost there – you only have two more days of this crazy movement challenge (though I bet you have been secretly enjoying it!). Today you are going outside. Grab a ball if you have one and head out into your backyard. If you don't have a backyard, head to the nearest park. And if you don't have a ball, just head outside where there is space to run. Take your partner, your kids or your friends and if none of them are available, just go by yourself. Get outside and kick that ball, or play tag or hide and seek. Whatever it is, run around, laugh and have fun, just like you did when you were a kid.

Don't forget to add those three words to your list again.

Day 7

You have made it! The final day is here and to celebrate, you are going to have a dance party. Before work, at work or after work, take your playlist, or make another one, and go for it. Dance in the kitchen, in the living room, on the deck, even in the boardroom (if everyone has gone home, that is!). Dance like no one is watching. And then add another three words to your list.

There you go! That was seven days of movement, of exercise, and you didn't even have to join the gym. It really can be done.

Now have a look at all those words you have been recording. I am hoping, if you followed my challenge, that you have had a smile on your face from time to time, that you have had some fun, and that you are feeling a little happier. The words you have written should reflect this.

Your work colleagues may think you are a little crazy, but they are probably secretly wondering what you are up to. Why don't you create your own movement challenge for your team or office and see what fun you can have?

YOU NEED TO SLEEP!

Sleep is essential for good health. It is the time our body, particularly our brain, takes to repair, rest, store memory and prepare for the next day. I am sure I don't have to convince you that when you don't get enough sleep, you find thinking, working and living the next day so much harder.

Most of us need seven to eight hours of uninterrupted sleep each night. Some people cope just fine with as little as five hours, while others need at least ten hours. Either way, modern life tends to mean that most of us don't get enough sleep a lot of the time.

The impact of a lack of sleep

Aside from causing us to feel (and look!) terrible, a lack of sleep has significant effects on our brain functioning. There is a reason places like the Guantanamo Bay Military Prison Facility allegedly used sleep deprivation as a primary form of torture. In short, the ongoing effect of a lack of sleep sends us mad.

Most of us lawyers are not going without sleep entirely (although I do remember the occasional night at university when I was up all night to get an assignment in!). However, we often don't get enough sleep or have broken sleep.

Whether it is down to that phone buzzing beside you, those kids who just don't want to sleep through the night, or the thoughts that you just can't turn off, one of the biggest challenges we all face is consistently getting enough sleep to operate at our peak.

A lack of sleep has a significant effect on our brain and body, putting us at higher risk of heart disease and attack, high blood pressure, diabetes, anxiety and depression. A lack of sleep and depression almost feed each other – an ongoing lack of sleep may lead to depression and depression makes it much harder to sleep.

When we don't get enough sleep, our bodies release more and more cortisol, the stress hormone, which, again, makes us more susceptible to mental health conditions and further affects our ability to sleep.

If we don't get enough deep-sleep cycles during the night, our brain doesn't have the chance to consolidate our memories and we aren't, therefore, able to remember what we learned and experienced during the day.

A lack of sleep also increases our risk of obesity. Sleep helps maintain the right balance of hormones that monitor our hunger. When we don't have enough sleep, we start to feel hungrier than we need to. The amount of insulin in our body is also affected and sleep deficiency can mean higher than normal blood sugar levels. This increases our risk of diabetes.

When we sleep, the hormones that support healthy growth and repair of bones and muscles, cells and tissues are released. A lack of sleep means these hormones are not released in the volumes they should be, which is bad news for our body.

And then there is our immune system – when we don't sleep well, our immune system doesn't work well and we find ourselves catching every illness that comes through the door of the office (or our home!).

So the message is pretty simple, really. If we don't get enough sleep, our Porsche-like bodies don't operate as the high-performance cars we need them to be. We find ourselves struggling through work, making errors, unable to be productive and being irritable and difficult along the way. All in all, not good news for any lawyer wanting to be happy.

How do I get enough sleep?

When it comes to sleep, like diet and exercise, it is one of the things that we give little priority to as we try to 'fit it all in'. We stay up late and get up early and often don't rest well in between.

When it comes to maximising your sleep, here are a few tips:

- Try to get to bed at the same time each night and rise at a similar time each day (making sure there are around eight hours in between those times!). If you want to be up by 6am each morning, you need to be in bed, eyes closed and snoring, by 10pm.

- Give your body and your brain a chance to wind down at night. Anyone who has children knows that bedtime can be such a challenge – they protest, delay and do all they can to avoid the inevitable, so we parents create bedtime routines for them so they know what is coming and what is expected. Given that we humans are creatures of habit, the routines we create for children will work for you too. So create yourself a bedtime routine that you can stick to, one that has you calming your mind and body at least thirty minutes prior to sleep.

- Avoid having your phone, TV, iPad and all those other great, beeping devices next to you. Turn them off so you can drift off in peace. Unless you are a criminal lawyer who is really willing to get up and head to the cells at 2am, I encourage you to leave email alone until the morning. Even if you are that criminal lawyer, your client is clearly not going anywhere until the morning, so as long as your voicemail reminds them to 'say nothing', surely you can deal with it tomorrow.

When I was researching this book, I surveyed hundreds of lawyers from Brisbane and beyond about their views on what was driving unhappiness. The one thing that came up consistently was the expectation that we are contactable all the time. Email, social media and the digital world have completely changed the practice of law. In some ways, this is for the better. However, a significant downside of this fast-paced technology is the inability many of us have to 'shut off' – to turn the phone or email off when we are out of the office. If ever there were a time to turn off your digital media, it is night time, when you are with your friends, family or in bed. Just turn it off and see how much better you feel.

- Avoid stimulants like caffeine and alcohol for at least five hours before bed (yes, I know you love a nightcap, but while alcohol may help with the getting to sleep part, it does nothing for your body or brain either during sleep or the next day).

- Keep your bedroom dark, make sure your bed is comfortable and try to avoid reading or watching TV or Netflix in bed. These are my vices so I understand if you can't do the last bit. If you just have to read or watch something before bed, try to keep it light.

What you eat, the amount of exercise you do and the amount of sleep you get are the central building blocks of your happiness. These three things feed into each other. In other words, the better you eat, and the more exercise you do, the better you sleep. Of course, the worse you sleep, the greater chance there is that you will eat poorly and skimp on exercise.

When it comes to your health, the stereotypical day in the life of a lawyer shows law to be one of the most unhealthy occupations possible. I have lawyer friends who regularly start work at 3 or even 4am. They push through until close to midnight. They barely leave their office and I am quite sure they eat takeaway all day (if they eat at all!). They do no exercise other than walking from their car park to their desk and to the bathroom a few times each day.

If this is you, please stop now. I promise you, no matter how effective you think you are, all of the science in the world tells us that you are not operating as a high-performance Porsche but merely a 1970s Datsun. I know the partners at your firm might all look at me like I am crazy, but you cannot be producing high-quality legal work on less than three hours sleep a night, seven nights a week. It is no use telling me that you will catch up on the weekend.

The first key to being a happy lawyer is to look after your own health. You have to make this a priority – no one else will. If you are working somewhere where health is not a priority, then start considering what is more important to you. We only live once, so we need to live the best life we can. You cannot be living your best life if you are constantly tired, are overweight, never go outside and use alcohol, nicotine or other substances to get yourself through.

Start right now. Make your health your number one priority and you will be on your way to being the happy lawyer you deserve to be.

"

Eat to nourish, fuel and heal
your body. Move because your
love your body, not because
you hate it. Your body is not
an ornament, it was designed
to be used. It loves to run,
stretch, swim, lift, jump and
sweat. If you do not use it,
you will lose it.

- MEL STOREY-SCOTT, SOLICITOR, BRISBANE -

We are the directors of our own mindset.

We may not be able to control outside factors, we can't stop bad things happening or ensure our path is pebble-free, but

— we can —

choose how we react

to the annoying jabs, the pain and discomfort.

—LISA MESSENGER —

A is for Attitude

When it comes to happiness, your attitude is the next important attribute on my list. For me, attitude encompasses a few things:

How you think.

What you do.

How you feel.

It is much easier to change how you think or what you do than it is to change how you feel. But where so many of us get stuck is that we focus on trying to change how we feel without making any shift in how we think or what we are doing.

Those lawyers whom I consider happy have a particular attitude towards their life. They have a positive mindset. They actively practise kindness, gratitude and empathy and, when faced with a challenge, they are able to take a deep breath and tackle it head on. These happy lawyers are quick to take when they haven't lived up to their own expectations, but they rarely judge the decisions or actions of others. They are compassionate, well-meaning and very mindful.

Let's look at how you can cultivate this happy lawyer attitude.

THE MAGIC IN MINDFULNESS

The key to changing my approach to life was slowing down.

Each year, I like to set a few goals around New Year's – some for me, some for my business, some for our family and then usually one crazy, fun, probably unachievable goal, just because! (This year's was to become a brand ambassador for my favourite Australian clothing label: Gorman.)

Last year, a goal I set became a value that I tried to live my whole year by – 'slow down'. This didn't mean moving slower; it meant focusing on being in the moment, and enjoying my life for what it was that day, not always thinking about what would be happening tomorrow or the next day.

Those two words, 'slow down', became my mantra for 2015, so much so that I have carried them into 2016 and still say them to myself about five times a day.

I expect your day-to-day life is a little like mine – getting up early, organising my daughter for the day, getting her out and me to work, organising my team at work, doing my own work, trying to fit the things I love in the middle before a meeting or two after work, exercise and, hopefully, getting home before my daughter hits her bed. I then spend what little time I can with my husband before pulling the computer out once he heads to bed and finishing off a few more things before my eyes start to close. Your daily life no doubt comes with your own levels of 'busy', so I encourage you to try the 'slow down' mantra too.

When you feel things are getting frantic (for me, it's about fifty times a day!), the secret is to stop. Just stop whatever you are doing and be still. Take at least three slow, deep breaths and say, 'Slow down.' Now, you don't have to slow down physically; the point is to slow your mind down to be focused on one thing only – what you are doing right now, nothing more and nothing less. Slowing down in life means that you can live mindfully and appreciate the present.

'Mindfulness' has become a buzzword of late, applicable in so many aspects of life, and I am a huge advocate.

It was described by one of its modern teachers, Jon Kabat-Zinn, as: 'paying attention in a particular way; on purpose, in the present moment, and non-judgmentally.'

So much of our negative mindset comes from worrying about things that may never happen. Rather than thinking about what we are doing now, we worry about all the things we still need to do – that mile-long to-do list and the chores you forgot to get done at home. So much of our personal stress comes from worry, but that worry can be contained if we just focus on the here and now.

Ten years ago, 'multitasking' was the buzzword. The story was that men couldn't multitask but women could – in fact, we wore our multitasking badge with honour! Then, one day, I sat through a risk management session with our local legal insurer where it became very apparent to me that multitasking was one of the biggest causes of insurance claims against lawyers. That was the end of multitasking at work for me!

At work, it is becoming harder and harder to concentrate on doing one thing at a time. Between colleagues, clients, phones, emails, messages and the myriad forms of online contact, the capacity to sit and do one task, mindfully, on purpose, almost feels like a luxury we will never have again.

So here I am to challenge you! Your mindset – your capacity to focus on what you need to do, to be mindfully present – is an essential part of your happiness, so you need to start to create your own rules or rituals to ensure that you can cultivate a positive one.

For me, email has been one of the biggest challenges when it comes to my work. Emails seem to be sent with an expectation that the person receiving them is sitting with their inbox at the ready, with nothing else to do but respond to the sender the minute it hits. And, sadly, some of us are doing just that. At least, that was the situation I found myself in last year. Every day, I was receiving 200 or more emails. If each email took me only a minute to answer, it was still more than three hours of my work day spent on emails rather than proactively dealing with my own 'to dos'. I found myself feeling constantly behind, never really on top of things and worrying all the time about items left in my inbox that I had not yet managed to get to. I had to find a better way of working or I was going to go crazy.

My answer was a combination of things. I made a rule not to open my inbox until I had done what I came to do when I sat in front of my computer, and at the same time I had my PA manage my inbox so that I could mindfully concentrate on the things I really needed to get done. This started to solve the problem, but even as I type there are over 400 'read' but not actioned emails sitting in my inbox.

Here are a few other tips and tricks I have found that helped me with managing email:

- Closing down the inbox on my computer for periods (an hour, for example) so that I can focus on a single task.

- Turning off the notifications sound both on my computer and iPhone.

- Only responding to email at certain times of the day.

- Using autoresponders so that people know when they can expect a response and giving them an alternative option if their matter is urgent – this is particularly helpful if you, like me, have days where you might be out of your office, in Court or at a mediation or course, and need to focus on the matter at hand.

- Being clear with my clients from the outset that email is not always the best way to reach me and it's better to use the good old telephone!

- And perhaps the most important one for me – encouraging my team to avoid internal emails altogether. I run a small team and it is about three steps between each office door. I much prefer the conversation to the email and this has really helped lessen the unnecessary emails in my inbox, while at the same time ensuring I can actually talk with the people I work with.

- Another tip that I have recently discovered is using apps such as Trello (www.trello.com) or Slack (www.slack.com) to manage your internal communication. I discovered Trello only a few months ago and it has changed my life. It enables you to set up online to-do lists with shared access. We are using Trello in our office to project-manage different parts of our business (in fact, the plan for my book was all in

a Trello board, which has made the writing process so much easier).
I am yet to start using Slack but I have many friends running inter
national businesses in different time zones who swear by Slack, so
perhaps check it out if you are like me and don't have a practice
management system that does all of this for you.

Mindfulness practice offers so many benefits. If you can train your mind to
stop running away from you, to focus on one task at a time and to enjoy that
task – whatever it may be – I promise you will feel calmer, more connected
and happier. It is easy to incorporate mindful practices in your daily life (you
don't even have to meditate if you don't want to!).

Take a few breathing breaks

Slowing down your breath, and purposefully breathing in and out while you
just focus on your breath, is a great way of settling your mind. This is the
perfect thing to do if you feel your thoughts are starting to run away from
you, and it is also a great technique to use just before you have to rise to your
feet in Court. Building a few breathing breaks into your day is a great way of
bringing your mind back to the moment, while, of course, filling your body
with lots of great oxygen. If you find yourself sitting at your desk for more
than an hour, then stand up, stretch your arms to the ceiling, close your eyes
and take at least three really slow, deep breaths – in through your nose and
out through your mouth. Try to let go of your thoughts and try to just focus
on your breath. If you focus on the movements in your body and how your
body feels, you should be able to calm that busy mind. If you can manage to
do this for a minute at a time, it works like a dream.

Create a mindful touchpoint

As we go about our days, we pass so many beautiful things without even realising it. By choosing a touchpoint, you can train your brain to bring you back into the moment, and to see the beauty around you. A touchpoint can be anything and you may have more than one. Sunsets, sunrises, the smell of coffee, a child's smile, a photograph, a saying, even music can all be touchpoints. Try to find something you will come across each day. When you do, it should bring a smile to your face as your brain is reminded that, even in the busyness, there is beauty.

Focus your mind on curiosity, not judgment

Everywhere we turn, we are faced with judgment. Whether it be on social media, on our TVs or in our newspapers, we spend our days judging the lives, decisions and beliefs of others, but to what end? Curiosity is a beautiful human trait best expressed by young children. I look at my daughter at the ripe old age of four and watch as she explores the world – she has no judgment, no fear, and everything around her is a new, exciting and curious experience to be explored and understood. If only we could recreate some of that childlike curiosity in our lives as adults.

We are curious when we poke around with wonder, really trying to work something out and better understand it. Just ask, 'Why?' Why is a person thinking, saying, feeling or doing something that we perhaps don't agree with? Understanding may not mean that you agree with an opinion, a belief or a decision, but curiosity will help you do your best to see the world from another person's point of view. When we train our brains to be curious before being judgemental, we better understand the things being said and done around us and are more mindful in our dealings with others.

Mindfulness practices are being shown to reduce stress, and improve well-being and resiliency. I expect we will all see a much broader dialogue in the future about incorporating mindfulness into our daily legal work.

When you think about it, it is really common sense. If we are able to focus in the moment, we bring our whole brain to an activity. Given that law is such a 'thinking' job, it surely makes sense that we need to have all of our attention on a case, a conversation or a document when it is presented to us. Meanwhile, outside your work, there is so much to be said for being mindful with your family and friends.

I have a friend and mentor who is a master at this. He is one of the busiest people I know, but when you are in a conversation with him, it is like you are the only person on this earth. The feeling this gives me is so powerful in a world where everyone seems to be only half paying attention.

I have found mindfulness useful at work, but even more useful at home. By focusing on being in the moment with my daughter and husband, I can enjoy every moment for what it is, instead of worrying about what might or might not be happening tomorrow. Children are a great help in implementing mindful practices – they have a wonderful ability to see beauty in all sorts of crazy things! By slowing down, and paying attention to what you are doing in the moment, you are stopping your mind from being influenced by negative past experiences or jumping ahead to the future.

CHOOSE YOUR ATTITUDE

I am, by nature, an optimistic person, but it turns out most lawyers aren't. The pessimistic lawyer is never hard to come by. No doubt, they excel at their job given their natural ability to find problems well before they arise.

The challenge for the pessimistic lawyer is not to turn that pessimistic mind-set to their life beyond the cases on their desk.

Some of us are naturally more 'glass half full' than others, but optimism is something you can create. This is the beautiful thing about how we think. You are in charge of your own thoughts and you can change them, training your brain to think in a particular way and changing what you are doing. I don't mean in the career sense; I mean in the day-to-day, living your life, caught up in the hustle and bustle sense. If you can change your mind and be present, and change your actions to be consistent with that, you will be well on your way to achieving an optimistic outlook. When we feel rushed or disorganised, it is much harder to maintain optimism. By focusing on the moment – slowing down and being mindful – you give yourself the best chance to find the good in the challenge.

When it comes to being a happy lawyer, a positive, optimistic approach is key. Optimistic people handle stress better, get sick less and even live longer. Now, why wouldn't we want that?

We are in control of our own thoughts and, as such, we can choose to be more positive, more optimistic – to see the world as if it is always a glass half full.

Here are a few ideas to kick-start your positive attitude:

Be grateful

Each day, I take a moment to count my blessings, to pause and reflect on those things for which I am grateful. When things are going well, this is easy, but when things are tough, it is hard even to want to be grateful. Those are the times I find I need it most. Make gratitude part of your daily rituals. It will take no more than a minute but can be a lot of fun, particularly if you get your kids and partner or friends and colleagues involved.

A great way of starting this is using a gratitude journal or jar. At the end of each day, write down three things you are grateful for. I do this with my daughter each night as I put her to bed, saying simply, 'Tell me three great things that happened today.' The answers always bring a smile to my face. Try it with yourself, your partner and your kids, and you might be surprised at the fun you can have. Writing it down means you will have a lovely record to look back on when times are not so easy.

Positive psychology research consistently associates gratitude with greater happiness. Gratitude helps us feel more positive emotions, see the good in any experience, manage adversity and, importantly, build strong relationships.

So why not give it a go?

Be kind

Kindness is a trait I live and breathe. It takes so little to demonstrate kindness and it is certainly something I cherish in return. Kindness and happiness go hand in hand for me. Kindness may be different for each of us, but I sense it comes back to good, old-fashioned values – having good manners, treating others fairly and with respect, being curious but not judgemental, and remembering that we never really know what is happening in another person's life. When people are challenging me, I adopt the motto 'kill them with kindness', and it works.

Research has also shown a link between kindness and happiness. Happier people are kinder and kinder people are happier. By engaging in random acts of kindness, you can improve your own happiness levels.

So go on, get out there and be kind to everyone around you!

Find opportunity in difficulty

We lawyers are not great when it comes to making mistakes. In fact, I have worked with many a lawyer who will swear to you they have never made a mistake in their life. Now, for one, that is just not possible, and for another, mistakes aren't a bad thing – they are the breeding ground of great opportunities.

Working with divorcing couples every day, I have seen the wonderful opportunities that come from such periods of challenge. So many of my clients go on after their divorce to form great new relationships, start new jobs or even build new businesses, and but for their divorce – that moment that shook their life and turned it upside down – they would never have ended up where they are.

Look for the silver linings. You will make mistakes and you will face periods of challenge in your life, but if you can train your brain to look for the learnings and the opportunities, you will start to deal with these moments differently.

Reflect

Perhaps you or someone around you has found themselves making an error of judgment. If you take the time daily to reflect, to come at the world from that place of curiosity, you will find yourself much better able to deal with challenges. We have all done things from time to time that we are not proud of, and we will all do more things in the future that may not come from our best selves. The action is not the issue; it is our ability to pause and reflect upon, take responsibility for, and learn from these moments that will keep us pushing forward on our path of happiness.

Surround yourself with positive people

Whether you are an introvert or an extrovert, the people you spend your time with will have an impact on how you think and feel. If you can't find great, positive people in the law, then look outside it. Reconnect with old friends or find new ones; just try to find positive people to spend your time with. Optimism is contagious.

The other side of this coin is just as important. Negative people, those who just want to pull you down, will prevent you from finding that optimistic attitude and overall happiness. This means we might need to say a kind 'goodbye' to some of the people in our lives, or at least be aware of their impact on our mindset and limit our time with them.

Manage your own expectations

Let's be realistic, the life of a lawyer is hard work. It often involves long days at a desk, little positive communication with others and many thankless tasks as we go about trying to mop up the mess in other people's lives. I have come to believe that many young lawyers struggle because their expectations of what 'lawyer life' will look like are a little too far removed from reality.

Law is full of high achievers. Many students go into law school having been top of their class, only to be surrounded by hundreds of others who are brighter, smarter and faster than they are. In the workplace, you are surrounded by people who are better than you at all sorts of things. This can be a little soul-destroying, if you let it. But just think – our Judges didn't rise to the top of their trade in the first two years of their careers. They worked hard for many years and are still working hard, learning and getting better and better. Manage your expectations and follow their example if you want to reach the top.

I encourage you to 'run your own race'. Don't worry about what those around you are doing – focus on you, set your own goals and manage your own expectations accordingly. My test for myself is what I call the 'Am I proud?' bar. When it comes to my life, when all is said and done, can I honestly look at myself and what I have done and feel proud? As long as I feel proud, I don't mind what anyone else thinks. I am running my own race, in my own time, at my own pace, and at the end of it all, I only have myself to answer to.

If you are new to this career or perhaps still studying, try to be real with yourself from the outset. There is so much to learn. Embrace that and enjoy it. Don't be disappointed if you're not made partner by the time you're thirty.

Have a sense of humour

The happy lawyers in my life are always the first to have a laugh, particularly at themselves. They don't take themselves too seriously. They appreciate that life is full of bigger issues and use humour as a great tool to get themselves through. Never underestimate the power of a good laugh. Remember that, aside from exercise, laughter is one of the quickest ways to get a release of endorphins into your body.

If you change how you think and what you do on a daily basis, you will change how you feel. A happy lawyer has a positive attitude. They aim to be mindfully present. They live in the moment and look for the good in any situation. They appreciate what they have rather than always looking for what they don't.

Health is the first building block of a happy lawyer and attitude is the second. Without your health, all the positive thinking in the world won't make you happy. But once you have your health under control, your mindset will make all the difference.

"

Finding something to be happy about each day and enjoying each day for what it is has made a huge difference to my overall happiness.

- FREYA GARDON, SOLICITOR, BRISBANE FAMILY LAW CENTRE -

'If you let go
of passion
— and follow —
your curiosity,
your curiosity might just
lead you
to your passion'.

— ELIZABETH GILBERT —

P is for Passion

Now we are onto the fun stuff! You should be feeling healthier because you have begun your movement challenge. And your attitude must be pretty positive – otherwise you would have given up reading by now! It's time to move on to my two favourite attributes of the happy lawyer – passion and purpose.

I have toyed with the correct order of these two over and over. Does purpose come before passion or passion before purpose? I have come to the conclusion that they are each as important as the other.

Let's start with passion!

WHAT IS YOUR PASSION?

This may seem like a funny question with an obvious answer, but when I sat down to think about it, I found it harder than I thought I would to describe just what having passion in life really means.

We often associate the word passion with the work that we do, but for many of us, our passions lie well outside our careers. And this is, I think, where many of us get stuck.

When I talk about 'passion', I am referring to the strong emotion that we all have inside us for a certain something or things in life.

My passions are chocolate, the creative arts (making all sorts of things!), swimming, dancing and writing. If I could spend all of my days creating sparkly objects that mean nothing, writing books like this one or dancing, dancing, dancing, I would be a very, very happy person (save that I might be broke…).

My passions are not necessarily connected to me being a lawyer (I know, shock horror – can you believe I just said that?). But there is no doubt that I use my career in the law as a tool to enable me to explore many of my passions in life (even dancing, but that is a story for another day).

It's okay to have more than one passion (and for most of them to have nothing to do with the law!). Just remember, our passions are those things that we can get entirely lost in; they are all-consuming, fun and make you feel happy.

If you are struggling to reconnect with your passions in life, then take your mind back to your childhood. What did you love to do?

Ask yourself, 'If money were no object, how would I spend my day?'

Most of us joke that we would move to a deserted island, which I imagine would be great for about a month before our driven lawyer-brain became bored. So imagine you have done the island thing and are now back home. What would you do with your day?

If money were no object I would do...

....

....

I would feel...

....

....

I would spend my time with...

....

....

I would go...

....

....

I would see...

....

....

What have you found? What are some of the themes? Are you already making time for some of these passions?

FINDING THE TIME TO DO THE THINGS THAT YOU LOVE

Just like when it comes to your health, I expect you are going to tell me that you don't have time to fit any of those passions in. Life is already too busy, too full, and there is no time for anything else, right?

Wrong! If you want to be a happy lawyer, you are going to have to find the time to fit your passions into your life – every day of your life, in fact. And with a little bit of thought, planning and purposeful action, you can do it.

Let's take creativity, for example – one of my deepest passions. I am happiest when I am creating. Right now, I have just enjoyed three days of intense writing, probably more than twelve hours each day, and I couldn't be happier. I sent my family on a mini break, set my computer up at our dining room table, made sure I stocked our fridge and freezer with yummy essentials, and sat down to write this book. I have been in a deep creative dream for three whole days and it has been a blast. But it is coming to an end, fast! It is now Monday, my inbox is going 'ping' every minute, and my capacity to drown in creative joy is diminishing by the second.

So, here's the thing, I have always been a creative soul. As far back as I can remember, I was making and dreaming up the strangest of creations, but over the past few years, I have entirely embraced the creative part of me and allowed it to flow wholeheartedly into my work. Whether it be writing for my blog, decorating my office, creating social media posts and brochures, or even picking my outfit in the morning, I get to be creative in some way every day, and this goes a long way to making me happy.

Now, the idea of writing a book for three days straight may make you want to stick pins in your eyes, but that is entirely okay. What is the thing that you just love to do? What is it that means the world may as well stop around you, as you are so consumed by your task and how it makes you feel that nothing else matters? Tell me what that is. That is your passion.

I have lawyer friends who have a deep passion for exercise (I am thinking of three in particular, two of whom are now Judges!). They could run, ride and swim for three days without stopping and would be bouncing off the walls when they're done. Now that is passion. Each of them has worked their passion for exercise and sport into their days – they run or ride to and from work, are up early to get to the pool, or throw the joggers on over lunch. They love it, so they do it every day, and they are clearly very healthy and happy as a result.

I have another lawyer friend who loves fashion. So much so, she has started a hugely successful fashion blog, sharing outfits she finds and all things fashion. She now has a booming business alongside her daily law career. She finds the time because she loves it and it makes her happy, while remaining a great lawyer.

One of the lovely lawyers who works with me is a passionate gardener. Her garden could feature in magazines the world over and could also feed a small village with the fruit, vegetable and herbs it produces. She is a great lawyer and works so very hard, but every day she spends at least an hour in her garden, because it's her passion.

I love nothing more than talking to lawyers about their passions. It is when you really get to learn about who they are as people.

We all have passions, but some of us are more courageous than others in incorporating them into our daily life. To be happy, you must find a way to work those passions into every day, particularly into your work day.

BRINGING YOUR PASSIONS TO WORK AND YOUR WORK TO YOUR PASSIONS

Are you ready for another challenge? This time we have a passion challenge. When it comes to being a happy lawyer, I am firmly of the view that you need to integrate your passions into your work in some way, almost every day. So let's give it a whirl!

Before we begin, you will need to grab that list of passions from before: What do you love doing? What do you get lost in? What brings a smile to your face? Write them all down here.

If money wasn't an issue I would love to spend my time...

1 ....

2 ....

3. ....

4. ....

5. ....

6. ....

7 ....

Working your passions into every day

Now you have that list, I want you to take a few moments and think about which of those passions you can work into every day.

So, for me, dancing is a passion. It clearly has nothing to do with my day job (unless I am organising a charity pantomime or being asked to join 'Dancing CEOs' again … oh yes, I have done both), so I overcome this by starting my day with a great song playing and my daughter and I jumping around in the kitchen. If my husband is home, he has to join us too. That three minutes of crazy, fun, silly dancing makes me feel great and is just so much fun!

So what is it for you? What do you love that you can do every single day? Have a look at that list and choose one thing (or more than one thing if you can). Your challenge this week is to fit this into every day, no matter what.

Whatever it is, you need to fit it in today. It might be before work, after work or during work – it doesn't matter when – today, you just need to do it. And once you have done it today, you need to do it tomorrow, the next day and the day after that too.

Finding passion in your work

This part of the challenge may be a little harder. This time, we are going to look at exactly which bits of your job as a lawyer connect with your passions. To help with this, let's try another list. This time, I want you to think about the parts of your job that bring you joy – the bits you just love! Now if, as you are reading this, your mind is saying, 'Nothing! I don't enjoy anything about my job!' then we have some digging to do.

When I was at my lowest in 2013, I also felt there was nothing about my job that I enjoyed. I couldn't see the wood for the trees, and the idea that something about my job could bring me joy seemed foreign. However, when I stopped and made myself really do this, and write a list of the things about my job that I did enjoy (even when I felt that there was nothing), it was progress in my shift to happiness. The reason why may be obvious: As soon as I was able to work out which parts of my job I loved, I was able to start purposefully sculpting my career to give me the best opportunity to do those bits more.

So, some of the bits I love about being a lawyer are:

- The capacity to connect with people, hear their stories, and be part of one of the most challenging times in their lives and support them through it.

- The creativity inherent in constructive negotiation – when you can really think, plan and sculpt options that have the potential to benefit both parties in a dispute.

- The talking – I love talking to my clients and my colleagues, sharing stories and learning about them.

- The learning – I love that I am always learning and there is still so much more to learn.

- The variety that comes with my job – that no two days are the same.

- The business of running a business.
  So give this a go yourself. What are the bits of your job that bring you

joy? Do take some time to play with this one. If you are struggling, like me three years ago, then start listing the bits that you don't enjoy first – if nothing else, it helps to work out what you don't like about your job so you can minimise those parts of it.

The parts of my job that I just love are…?

1   ....

2   ....

3.   ....

4.   ....

5.   ....

6.   ....

7   ....

Now you have that list, I want you to go back a few pages to that list of passions. Take a few moments and have a look for any connections between the parts of your job that bring you joy and your passions. Many of my passions sit in a creative space, so it is no surprise to me that when I am working in a creative way as a lawyer, I am my happiest. What is it for you.

Parts of work I really enjoy

....

....

....

....

....

....

....

....

....

....

....

....

My Passions

....

....

....

....

....

....

....

....

....

....

....

....

Once you have identified the parts of your work that you can connect with one of your passions, the next part of your challenge is to focus on just how you can do more of the bits that you love. I call this playing to your strengths. Now, I appreciate that not everyone works for themselves, and you may not be able to suddenly stop doing the parts of your role that you don't like and just do the bits you love. But let me be clear, I still do a whole lot of things every day in my work that fall into the 'don't like very much' category. It's a utopian exercise to imagine that you could ever have a job where every part of it brought you joy (if you do have such a job, can you please let me know what it is!).

What I have done these past few years is purposefully and actively focus on ways to ensure that I do more of what brings me joy at work. This has meant more writing, moving almost entirely away from litigation, doing more teaching and mentoring, and talking a lot with clients and colleagues. I have applied a mindful approach to the active pursuit of opportunities that enable me to have more joy in the work that I do.

So take a few moments to really think about what you do – which bits do you really enjoy? There might be things that you want to do that you are yet to try; add those to the list too. Once you work out just which bits of your work you really enjoy, you can start to set some clear goals around how you can create more of these in every work day. So this time go back to that list of things that bring you joy and work your way back through to think about what you can do this week, this month and this year to make sure you have more of that in your work week.

I really love or enjoy..

1 ....

2 ....

3. ....

To do more of this I will...

This week: 1 ....

                2 ....

                3. ....

This month: 1 ....

                2 ....

                3. ....

This year: 1 ....

                2 ....

                3. ....

A FEW OTHER IDEAS FOR BRINGING YOUR PASSIONS TO WORK

When your passions sit well outside your work, you might be thinking that you just can't bring them with you. But I disagree. You really can – it's just about thinking creatively (and sometimes a little outside the box!).

An example is my friend Fiona Caulley, a fellow family lawyer but mad 'foodie'. Fiona is one of the great people in my life. She loves food and she always has the best restaurant recommendations. Food and family law clearly do not have a direct correlation, but Fiona and the team at her firm here in Brisbane have morning tea every day (Yes, that's right – EVERY DAY!). Every morning, they share a chat over some sort of scrumptious, healthy, gluten- and sugar-free treat. This small moment each day enables Fiona to connect with one of her passions, while at the same time going a huge way to building an inclusive, supportive and open culture in her firm.

Let's imagine you also have a passion that revolves around food – why don't you try bringing something you have baked or created to work with you and sharing it with your colleagues, perhaps even a client? I love to have delicious snacks in difficult meetings, particularly with clients.

Perhaps being outdoors in nature is something that is a passion for you. Why don't you try taking some of that work you have to do and sitting outside, somewhere green or perhaps by the water? See what that change of scenery does for your happiness.

Finding your passions and working them into your day shouldn't be arduous, so go on, have some fun, and find a way to get some of those passions into your daily life as a lawyer! It's easier than you think.

"

Wouldn't it be great if we could share our passions? Let others in on it. Don't forget the passions you don't even know about yet. Leave room for expansion.

- CHRISTINE GRANT, GRANT AND ASSOCIATES BRISBANE -

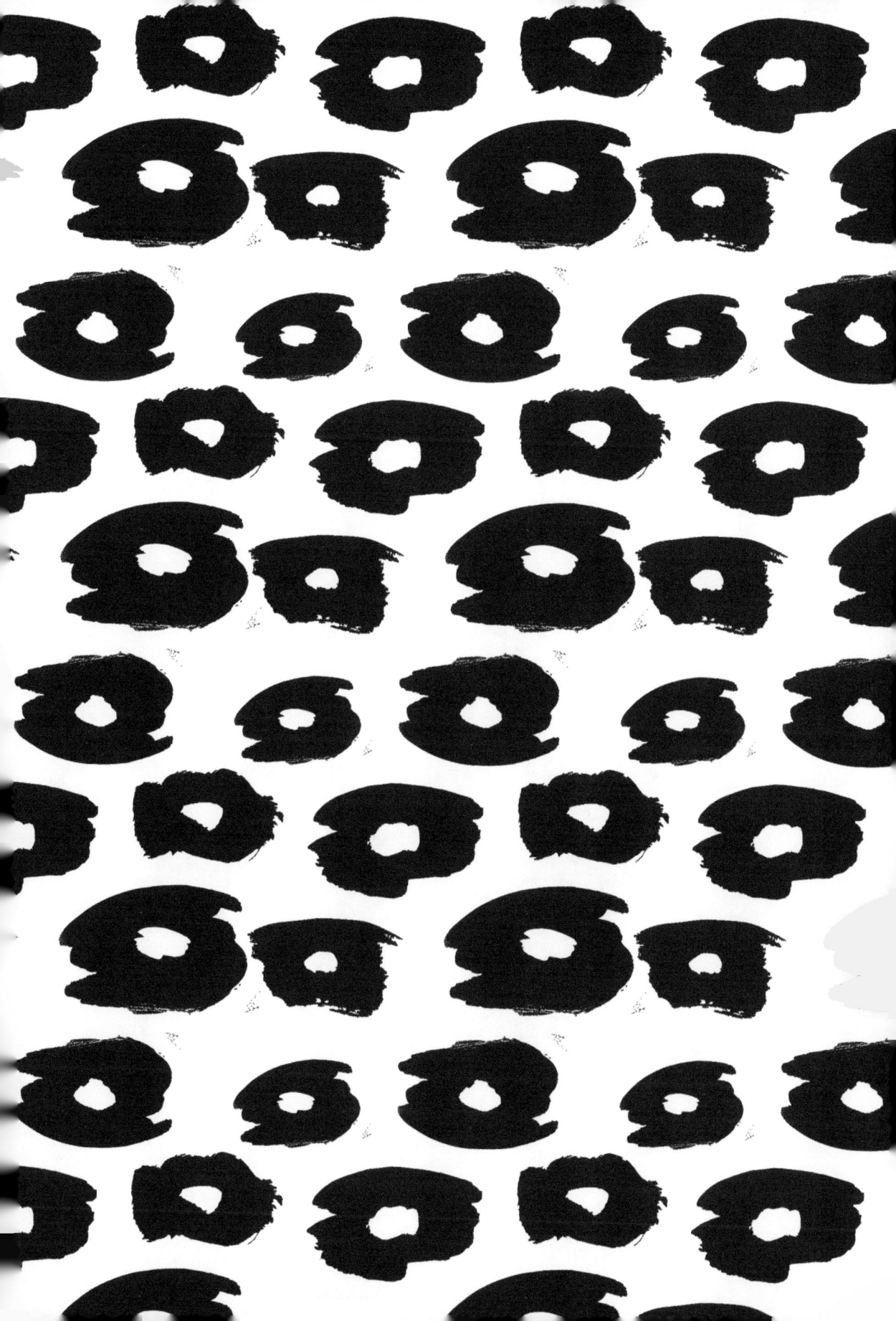

Pursue the things you love doing and then do them so well that people can't take their eyes off of you

— MAYA ANGELOU —

P is for Purpose

There are, no doubt, a lot of similarities when it comes to talking about passion and purpose. The main difference for me is this – passion is about a 'what' and purpose is about having a 'why'. To be truly happy, I think you need both.

THE IMPORTANCE OF KNOWING YOUR WHY

Simon Sinek is someone I follow, learn from and would love to accidentally meet one day! He is a powerful business thought leader who is best known for a TED talk he gave some years ago on the power of knowing your 'why'. Simon suggests that in the modern world of online business, information overload and big faceless brands, it is more important than ever to be able to articulate and be clear on why you do what you do.

He suggests that we are all inspired by 'the why'. This is your purpose. A great example of this concept in action can be seen in the story of Daniel Flynn, Justine Flynn and Jarryd Burns and their brand 'Thankyou'. If you are in Australia or New Zealand, there is a good chance you have at some stage in the past few years bought a 'Thankyou' product. In 2008, at the ripe old age of about nineteen, these three Australian university students decided their purpose in life was to tackle the world water crisis. At that time, over 900 million people didn't have access to safe drinking water on a daily basis, yet the Australian bottled water industry was worth an estimated $600 million a year.[12]

In July 2013, the group rebranded as 'Thankyou', and launched food, body care and then nappy and baby care ranges. The idea remains simple – 100 per cent of their profits go to funding projects around the world that tackle poverty.

Their why, their purpose, is clear – they intend tackling world poverty in their lifetime through social enterprise.

I have had the privilege of hearing Daniel and Justine share their story of the successes and failures of their first few years in business. These students were taking on the biggest retail corporations in the country. They had no end of roadblocks put in their way. However, their vision, their why – their purpose – means that they are not only selling bottled water, soaps and nappies; they are selling a step to a better world. When I am doing my grocery shopping, I can now buy all sorts of household basics from the Thankyou brand, and each time I do so, it's because these Australian teenagers had a vision, a purpose and a 'why' that inspires me to want to help them.

I know, as lawyers, we are not in the business of selling household products, and perhaps we are not about to solve world poverty either, but each and every one of us has our own purpose – our own reason for doing what we do. The hard bit is working out just what that is for you.

---

12   See https://thankyou.co/about for more information about the Thankyou products, purpose and brand

FINDING YOUR PURPOSE

Purpose comes from the heart and the gut; your sense of intuition. It is a deep feeling of doing something worthwhile, of being involved in something bigger than you. A lack of purpose is one of the drivers of unhappiness for so many of us in life, lawyers included.

When I surveyed my lawyer colleagues, the overwhelming driver for their choosing law in the first place came down to two things – the sense of helping others and the capacity to positively affect the lives of others. That is where their purpose sits, their why. Put simply, for many of us, our purpose is to make a difference in the lives of others.

You could have explored this purpose in so many different avenues in your life, perhaps even in a different career. When it comes to making a difference in the lives of others, law is merely your tool, as it is mine.

It took time and thought to find clarity around my purpose in law, but now that I have, it makes a lot of sense to stick with it! Knowing I am helping people through my chosen profession is one of the things I love about it.

CAN YOU REALLY LOVE WHAT YOU DO?

One of the most repeated sayings when it comes to 'loving what you do' comes, of course, from Confucius, who said, 'Choose a job that you love and you will never have to work a day in your life.' At some level, I think this is a wonderful philosophy, but I do wonder sometimes if it is realistic.

Any job, no matter how wonderful, comes with downsides. We mustn't focus too much on the fact that we don't love what we do all the time – it doesn't mean we are in the wrong job.

Sturt and Nordstrum are researchers based at the O.C. Tanner Institute whose work focuses on people who make a difference in this world. I figure they probably have something useful to say for us lawyers who fell into this career for that very reason. In an article on Forbes.com, they ask the question: Should we do what we love or love what we do?[13] They suggest that you can learn to find meaning and success in your current job, even if you don't love it. The secret is to change how you think about what you do.

Put simply, they suggest it's 'all about them, not you!'

They found a common theme in the workplaces and workers that they studied to be the fact they were focused on making a difference that someone else would love, not that they, the person performing the work, would enjoy.

'*They were focused on the recipient of their work—their customer, their colleague who depends on them, their leader who trusts in them, the community who expects their support, or others who benefit from their work.*'[14]

The challenge for us lawyers comes when we feel like the practice of law is doing anything but making a difference – this is when we feel our purpose is not being met and we can very quickly spiral into a state of unhappiness.

To pick up the thoughts of Sturt and Nordstrom, if we focus on the difference we are making in the lives of others and not on our own tasks, there is a good chance we will start to find that sense of purpose again. You make a difference for lots of people in and outside your career, often without realising it.

---

13   To see the full article go to http://www.forbes.com/sites/davidsturt/2015/03/13/do-what-you-love-or-love-what-you-do/2/#792af09fb2c3

14   As Above

The commercial grind of daily law practice can eat you up. Under pressure from six-minute units, billable targets and KPIs, it can be very hard to see the wood for the trees, to see that your hard work reviewing a 150-page document for five days really made any difference to anyone at all.

The trick is to find a way to ensure that your desire to help others, to make a difference in the world, is worked into each and every day and acknowledged. The simplest way to do this is to be mindful and pay attention to the signs that you have made a difference, rather than focusing on the moments when you haven't.

One such sign is a simple thank you, which is so easy to let pass you by. In my firm, in any given week, my team will receive emails, calls, letters and even gifts of thanks. When they come in, people smile, perhaps take a photo for the Facebook page, and then get on with their job.

But then an email or phone call comes in and it is a complaint about something we have done that did not go the way the client hoped. They are angry and difficult to manage. Before you know it, the whole office knows, and everyone is questioning why they chose a career in law.

Our human brains are hardwired to pay much more attention to negative, difficult and fearful moments in time. That is key to our survival – it is the basis of the flight or fight response. Our 'negativity bias' is inbuilt, so it is natural and normal for us to pay more attention to the bad than the good.

The problem, of course, is that we naturally put much more weight on that negative feedback than we do on the positive. I am sure you can easily tell me all the difficult, hard and negative things that occurred in the last week, but you would have to stop and really think to tell me the good stuff.

It is all about retraining your brain and changing how you usually think.

When the change is aligned with recognising that you are achieving your purpose, it really is possible to love what you do.

Your purpose challenge: Make a success board

Do you remember being at school and, at the end of each year, getting to take home this great book or folder of all the great things you did that year? It was like your personal success memento, which you could look back on to remind yourself of all the great things you did.

As kids, teenagers and students, we constantly received outward recognition for all the great things we did – trophies, medals, certificates and public praise. Then we started work, and save for the 'employee of the month award', there was unlikely to be anyone patting you on the back and saying 'good on you!' Because that is the joy of work – you are expected to do a good job and, as such, when you do, it probably goes unrecognised.

Unless you pause, pay attention and reflect upon your own successes, you cannot expect anyone around you to do that either. Herein lies the secret of a success board.

A success board is a visual reminder of some of the great things that you have done this week, last week, this year and last year. My own success board is this big pin-board in my office, crammed full of lots of random things – thank you cards, emails, quotes, photos, pictures from my daughter, letters from my team. Right next to me at my desk is a whole wall that says to me loud and clear, 'You are making a difference in all of these people's lives, so don't give up!'

If you want to be happy in your lawyer life, you need to find a way to retrain your brain to celebrate success. Success is not only winning awards; for most of us, it is reflected in that email from someone one morning that simply says 'thank you'. You probably get one a day and don't even realise, so now your job is to look for them.

If making a difference is part of your purpose, then I encourage you to take this challenge. Grab a big piece of cardboard (the type we used to use for school projects – head to the newsagent and hunt out the cardboard section). You are also going to need scissors and a glue stick.

Each day, I want you to print out or cut out an image, a quote, an email – anything that shows this day counts as a success. It might be a compliment, a thank you or a great result you worked hard to achieve. As successes happen, write them down, or take a photo, and glue them to your board. At the end of the week, you should have a perfect temporary success board that you can stick next to your desk to remind you that you are making a difference, even when it doesn't feel like it.

CONNECTING YOUR PURPOSE AND YOUR WORKPLACE

As I've mentioned, Simon Sinek is one of the business world's most famous authors and speakers when it comes to this notion of purpose. His TED talks are absolutely worth watching if you are struggling to understand your purpose.

Simon suggests that, as people, we are inspired by the 'why'. If a person or a business clearly articulates their 'why', their reason for doing what they do, then we cannot help but be inspired and follow them.

Simon's theory makes so much sense and when I embraced his

thinking and applied it in my business, I saw a significant and positive shift both in client and team engagement.

If you think of many of the great brands the world over that we are happy to be associated with, and buy from, they clearly articulate their purpose in everything that they do. Sinek often talks of the success of Apple as a brand. Apple, at the end of the day, is a technology company. They develop and sell computers, phones and similar products,just like many other companies. But Apple is different. They are clear on their purpose – to explore the intersection between great design and great technology that is easy to use. We, the consumer, are inspired by this. When we have an Apple product, we are carrying much more than a phone or a computer. We are buying a great design, an art piece that we are proud to carry around.

When it comes to lawyers and law firms, we are not the best at clearly expressing and marketing our purpose. A lot of lawyers, when I ask them why they do what they do, say to me something like, 'I know it sounds really corny, but I do this because I want to make a difference.' Most of them hide their purpose. They don't go proudly shouting it from the rooftops.

I appreciate this book is not about marketing, but I want to let you in on a little secret here, for both your business and your life. Whether you are a firm owner like me, a solo practitioner, an employed solicitor or an in-house lawyer or barrister – if you can get clear on why you do what you do and start articulating that to the universe with passion, you will be amazed at the impact this can have on you, your life, your career and your business.

At the end of 2013 when, by chance, I started a little blog called 'The Happy Family Lawyer', I kick-started a chain of events that I never imagined in my wildest dreams. Each week, as I shared in a short article my

thoughts, beliefs and feelings about life, love and heartbreak, I was articulating various aspects of my 'why' – why I do what I do as a divorce lawyer.
As soon as I started to do this, I observed a change in my team. Some people
moved on, but more and more wanted to join me. As I became confident and
clear on my own 'why', I began to attract people who shared my purpose – my
vision for managing the difficult thing that is divorce. And it wasn't just new
team members that I began to attract, but also a community of professionals
and people who shared my vision of changing the experience of divorce.

In law, we seem to be scared to share our purpose, our passions – what
we believe and why we do what we do. But so much of my happiness has
come as a result of me getting really clear on what I think, feel and believe
regarding why I do what I do. By then communicating that to everyone
around me, I have grown a team working in my firm that is equally on
purpose, friends who share many of my dreams, and clients who want to do
business with me because of my beliefs.

It may all sound a little 'woo woo', but there it is! A happy lawyer is
clear on why they do what they do, and they are proud to share that with
their team, their clients, their friends and the world. In turn, it makes the
business of lawyering much easier in the long run.

When it comes to passion and purpose, I encourage you to have lots
of both. Your passions are those things that you just love to do, so do them
every day. Your purpose is your 'why'. You are here because of the values and
goals that guide your decisions.

The two 'Ps' of the happy lawyer go hand-in-hand for me and are
equally important. It is up to you to find ways to create passion and purpose
in your everyday life. This is what it will take to find happiness as a lawyer.

"

Like perhaps many lawyers, I pursued a degree in law primarily because I wanted an ability to, through my career, 'make a difference.' Whilst seventeen-year-old me was seemingly naive, and I can only hope I've progressed a long way since then, that same desire still holds true. Be sure to take time to appreciate how far you have come, and be proud about it. I know that's something that makes me incredibly motivated, and happy.

- COURTNEY AITKEN, SOLICITOR, RUHL FAMILY LAW CENTRE -

Our deepest fear is that we are powerful beyond measure. We ask ourselves, who am I to be brilliant, gorgeous, talented, fabulous? Actually, who are you not to be? ...

Your playing small does not serve the world... And as we let our own light shine, we unconsciously give other people permission to do the same.

- MARIANNA WILLIAMSON -

Y is for You

On 23 October 2014, Justice Virginia Bell AC delivered the inaugural Tristan Jepson Memorial Foundation address. Her Honour delivered a powerful address and read the words of her former colleague, the Honourable Justice Mason, who said, when describing our role as lawyers:

'You will experience considerable pressure to conform to cultures of the firm, the set of chambers, the government department, and the faculty. This collective embrace is appropriate in so far as it educates, encourages and helps maintain proper professional standards. But never forget that as individuals you have the opportunity to project your values and your ideals into your chosen calling. Conversely, your personal wellbeing and the integrity of your life and belief system are vital to your ability to function as a legal practitioner.

You are a person first and a lawyer second.'

This speech and this statement have stuck with me since I first heard those words in 2014. That was about one year after I had begun my active pursuit of happiness. And to hear such successful members of our profession speak of the need to be 'a person first and a lawyer second' gave me the courage to be just that – to be Clarissa the whole person first, and a lawyer second.

Among all of the happy lawyers that I have come to know, I have found a common theme – they have all found a way to be themselves in the work that they do. They are authentically themselves everywhere they go. They are the same person both at work and at home and they want it no other way. They are just happy being themselves.

NO ONE IS YOU-ER THAN YOU!

When I started law school, I thought that being a lawyer involved smart black and navy suits, corporate offices with expansive views, probably earning lots of money and working really hard.

I took my first 'proper' job in a law office three years into my degree and very quickly realised that my expectations of what my career would be like and what it would actually be like couldn't have been much further apart.

My first day in a law office (if you ignore my couple of weeks working with a big firm in their mail room) involved a teeny tiny office, piles of files on the floor, no view and a lot of time at a photocopier that only worked some of the time.

I realised pretty quickly that my life as a lawyer was not going to be all that glamorous. And you know what? I was okay with that. I worked out pretty quickly that my job in those first few years was to learn as much as I could as fast as I could. For me, being in a tiny firm was the best place to be doing just that.

From the start, I was lucky enough to be working under a lawyer who did not necessarily fit into the lawyer stereotype. While there were times that his disorganisation drove me insane, there were many lessons I learned in those first few years that I will always be grateful for. I was encouraged early on to be independent, to be myself and to create my own career path.

We lawyers need to find a way to be comfortable in our own skin – to be authentically 'us'. Sure, there may be parts of our personality that don't fit best at work, but the thing is, the minute you allow yourself to be 'you', with all your strengths and challenges, you will be surprised how much happier you start to feel.

You are one whole person with so many valuable parts. Being a lawyer is only one part of who you are. Embrace that; don't try to isolate it. But, more importantly, don't isolate all the other great parts of you from the 'lawyer' in you.

No one is you-er than you. Rather than trying to spend your days being someone or something else, I encourage you to just be you – whoever that is!

But who am I? Identifying your values

As you have read through these pages, I suspect you have been doing a little bit of thinking about just who you are, what you love to do, your passions, your purpose, and the traits that you hope others associate with you.

At the core of each of us is a set of values or principles that we tend to live by, sometimes mindlessly. To be authentically you, it will be helpful to spend some time working out a few key facts about yourself. What are your core beliefs and values? What are some of the principles that guide your life? What are your priorities? And when all is said and done, what do you want to be known for in your career and in your life?

Our values determine our priorities and are often how we measure our success and happiness. If we consciously identify our values, we can make decisions and act in a way that is congruent with them, which gives us a far better chance of being happy.

The simplest way to identify your values is to look back on experiences in your life to pinpoint the times when you were the happiest or perhaps the most proud and fulfilled. Look at the times when you were most fulfilled during your childhood, then in adulthood, in your personal life and during your career. What were you doing? Where were you? Who was with you? What else about those times made you feel happy?

Try to find five occasions in your life where you have felt happiness, pride and fulfilment.

A moment from my childhood when I felt joy was...

....

....

A moment from my teenage years when I felt proud was...

....

....

A moment in my career when I felt fulfilled was...

....

....

A moment in my career when I felt happiness was..

....

....

A moment in my life I felt proud was...

....

....

Now, using these experiences, try to look for common themes – these will lead you to find your core values. Often, these are the values that you try to instil in your children.

Take a few moments to consider some of the values that are important to you. There are plenty of lists available online, so if you are struggling, consider Googling 'common core values'.

Here is a list that might help too.

Listening   Calm   Loyalty

Commitment   Involvement

Leadership   Intention   Authority

Humour   Laughter   Spirituality   Self-respect

Appreciation

Serenity   Excitement

Kindness   Vitality

Meaning

Honesty

Hope   Independence   Integrity

Knowledge   Diligence

Organisation   Freedom

Love   Nature

Mindfulness

Challenge   Influence

Personal growth

Movement

Order   Accountability   Development

Recognition   Passion

Friendship   Peace

Saving   Joy

Status   Planning   Power

Privacy   Relaxation

Wisdom   Openness   Inner harmony

Truth   Quality relationships

Self-confidence

Creativity   Intellectual challenge

Excellence   Strength

Potential   Tolerance

Sexuality   Adventure   Ethical practice

Receiving

Achievement   Structure   Decisiveness

Understanding   Compassion

Advancement

Curiosity

Beauty   Accuracy

Balance

Collaboration   Belief   Unity   Environment

Action   Efficiency   Community

Sharing   Connection

Safety   Determination

Physical challenge

Change   Admiration

Celebration   Growth

Rest   Equality

Choice

Forgiveness

Initiative   Entrepreneurship   Faith

Health   Trust

Family

Simplicity   Fame   Tradition

Generosity   Fun   Giving

Gratitude

Financial security

Confidence   Emotion

10 of my core values and principles

1   ....

2   ....

3. ....

4. ....

5. ....

6. ....

7   ....

8   ....

9   ....

10. ....

LIVE YOUR VALUES

Being helpful and kind are two values that are very important to me. So when people around me are unhelpful or unkind, I find myself getting very frustrated very quickly. I enjoy, therefore, being around people (clients included!) who are both helpful and kind, and I spend a lot of time talking with my daughter about the importance of these values.

When it comes to my firm, these are two traits that are embedded in the culture. I can look back now and see periods when there were members of my team who were unkind or unhelpful, and those are periods in my business life that I strongly associate with personal unhappiness.

The same will be true for you – when you and those around you share and operate in accordance with a similar value set, there is a strong chance you will be happier. I have found it really helpful to be clear about my own values – I think we know them innately, but articulating them, writing them down and taking a few moments to really think about them has helped me with my decision making.

When it comes to choosing a new team member for my business, I try to learn about some of their key values, to assess whether they will be a good fit. Meanwhile, the type of work I now do in Collaborative Practice tends to attract clients with some of the same core values as me.

You might find yourself with an opportunity to consider a new role at some stage. If you are clear on your own values, you can start to assess any new organisation to determine whether their values are likely to align with yours.

Prioritising family relationships is a core value for many of us. A common value misalignment I see with lawyers is when their work is regularly in conflict with this key value. Most of us need to, and do, enjoy our work; the difficulty arises when we find ourselves working all hours of the day and night or unable to disconnect from work when we do have downtime.

Being authentically you will be a whole lot easier if you are making decisions that are consistent with your core values. Perhaps more importantly, most of us find it much easier to be happy when we are surrounded by people who live their lives consistent with core values similar to our own. And, of course, a further extension of this theme is that you want to be working in an organisation that lives values that are consistent with your own.

PLAY TO YOUR STRENGTHS

The great thing about all of us is that we have strengths. Sometimes the trick is working out just what they are! You have probably picked up on a few of mine as you have been reading – creativity, openness, big-picture thinking – these are a few of the strengths that I tap into on a daily basis.

Back in 2013, when I started writing, I had no idea that so many wonderful opportunities were to come. From new friendships to new business to a whole community of wonderful people who are interested in my thoughts and feelings, my crazy decision to start writing has opened up a world of fun for me, all because I was playing to one of my strengths – creativity.

Let's take another example. My friend Kate Pateman is a family lawyer in sunny Townsville. Kate opened her own firm, one of the first specialist family law firms in Townsville, a few years ago. The legal landscape around her at the time was largely mid-sized, general practice firms that had held the marketplace in her town for the past 100 or so years. Kate is a vibrant, down-to-earth, fun person to have around – she is one of the funniest people I know! And, of course, she is a talented lawyer; I expect it is her personality and her capacity to connect with people that makes her such a great one. Kate's firm is a true expression of her – it is colourful, engaging and contemporary, and her two dogs run around the office all day! Kate has identified that her strength is her personality. Affable, fun, friendly, kind – she is all of those things, and her business is a tangible extension of those traits.

A more traditional example might be the lawyer who is a talented technician but perhaps not the creative extrovert. I have many a great lawyer friend who has pursued their career to the Bar because they are an expert in the detail of the law. These lawyers are playing to their strengths. They know their intellect is their significant strength and they take advantage of that strength in their work every day.

Take my friend Jennifer McArdle, a Barrister here in Brisbane. Jen is a wonderful lawyer who just loves to explore the law. She has a deep care for others, a kindness when it comes to her work and at the core she is a talented technician who can consume herself for hours in the detail of a Court case. Jen made the transition to the Bar a few years ago and has not looked back. She is now playing to her strengths – her love of fine detail and her broad and thorough knowledge, to name but two.

Do you think you're not really 'great' at anything? That's just not true. The thing is, when it comes to the stuff we are great at, we often don't even realise we have a natural talent for it – it just comes easily to us. For some reason, we tend to grow up thinking that being great at something must involve hours and hours of hard work, and so the stuff that just comes naturally can't be useful or valuable. There will be a long list of things that you are just great at, often without even having to think or try too hard. They are your strengths and you should play to them.

If you are struggling to work out just what you are great at, then ask the people you are closest to. Ask your family, friends and colleagues, 'What do you think are my three greatest strengths?' I love to ask this question in workshops with lawyers. We never take the time to consider what our natural strengths are. It almost always brings tears to my eyes and those of the person we are talking with when you hear one of their colleagues talk about just what makes them great. We don't spend enough time in this world reminding others of their strengths and it is, therefore, really powerful when we do.

Now have a go at the questions below to continue to work out just what makes you 'you'!

Three things I think I am naturally great at (my strengths).

1 ....

2 ....

3 ....

*Three things my partner/ great friend
has told me I am great at.*

1   ....

2   ....

3   ....

*Three things I just love to do that
are a part of my job now.*

1   ....

2   ....

3   ....

*Three things I just love to do
when I am not at work.*

1   ....

2   ....

3   ....

I am a dancer. I spent most of my childhood and teenage years at dance class for three or so hours after school, every day. I loved every minute of it and, in my twenties, there was a moment when I almost threw away my law career to pursue dancing. I have spent a lot of time thinking about the time and money my parents invested in my dance lessons when I was a child (it must have been a lot!), and I used to worry that it was all a waste. But over the past few years, I have come to see that those hours and hours of dance lessons are a huge part of what makes me 'me'. None of it was wasted. In fact, it is now the core of some of my biggest strengths as a lawyer. Dancing taught me discipline and determination and, at the same time, encouraged my creativity.

Every single thing you have ever done, whether good, bad, useful or, at the time, seemingly worthless, makes you 'you'. No one else has the same bundle of experiences, emotions, feelings and insights, and this is the best thing about the world! No one else can be you, so embrace it and run with it. It will be your biggest advantage, both in your career and in your life.

There are, of course, certain standards that we all need to operate by, so I am not suggesting you throw out your corporate wardrobe and embrace T-shirts and sandles for Court next week, but I am suggesting that you find a way of working 'you' into everything you do.

From the moment I opened my own firm, I focused on enabling my own strengths to feature in each day of my work.

I've spoken a lot about my love of creativity, writing, designing and generally making things beautiful. I've wholeheartedly embraced this in my firm, in the design and the branding, and in the way we work. As time goes on, I'm pushing those boundaries more and more, as I'm seeing that my ideal clients respond really well when I am authentically me.

I expect, if you are currently at the beginning of your career and working in a large firm, the notion of being yourself, bringing things that you love into work, and painting the boardroom walls seems so impossible right now.

But your career in law is likely to be a long one – it is a marathon, not a sprint, as they say. Sure, in the first six months, you might not be able to turn your office upside down and decorate it the way you want, but, over time, you will find your own place and you will work out just how you can be you in this profession; living your values, playing to your strengths and parading your passions.

DON'T BE AFRAID TO SHARE SOME OF YOUR STORY

The business world has changed more in these past ten years than, I think, in the many decades before, and this is never more obvious than in law. The way we now practise, thanks to the internet and the 'information age', is significantly shifting everything about our jobs at a rapid pace. Gone are the days of we lawyers being the holders of all legal knowledge. Now I can Google 'How do I get a divorce in Australia' and up jump myriad helpful resources that largely tell me the answer. Our role is changing fast and we need to be on the front of the wave of change if we want to survive.

We have seen the rise and rise of social media. That Facebook fad that seemed to hit a good few years ago now just won't go away, and so, finally, lawyers and law firms are starting to realise that to stay current, they need to change the way they think and work.

One of my greatest mentors regularly says, 'There has never been a better time to be in business!' and I wholeheartedly agree. But I think the way to do business now (in 2016 anyway) is very different from the way we did business when I first worked in law in 2000.

And here is where this authenticity thing really kicks in. Almost every encounter you have with a new client, new employer, new contact or new colleague starts with a Google search to see what you can learn about them and what they can learn about you. Our digital footprint is growing exponentially, despite lawyers being some of the slowest to embrace this new way of doing business.

Those lawyers and firms who are choosing to engage with the online world, particularly in the realm of social media, are learning quickly that having an authentic, defined and 'real life human' brand is essential to successfully embracing this new world of online marketing and business. Almost everyone everywhere is engaging on some level on a social media platform of some kind – even if it is just to watch our friends from the sidelines. And I am sure you will agree with me, those people that are themselves – actual, real people both online and offline – are the ones who encourage us to engage with them and, ultimately, do business with them.

So just in case you were questioning this notion of authenticity, I encourage you to embrace it not only because it is so much easier to be yourself than anyone else, but also because the sooner you do, the sooner you will be able to embrace and enjoy the modern online business world and develop a personal brand that will be your currency in the 'new law' world.

YOUR REPUTATION IS EVERYTHING

My first proper mentor in law taught me very quickly that your reputation is your most valuable asset as a lawyer. It takes many years of hard work build and can be lost in a second if we don't protect it vigorously. Our reputations can, of course, be constructed to a point, much like you can construct a personal brand. However, if you are trying to construct a brand or reputation that is not an authentic representation of who you really are at your core, then I suggest your hard work will probably be in vain.

Your reputation will become your brand, and it is your brand that you take with you wherever you go. The stronger and clearer your brand, the more respect and engagement you will command, with both employers and clients.

To build a strong reputation in law, I suggest you need to start by being a great lawyer. There is little point having a wonderful sales and marketing process, beautiful branding and stunning business model if, at the end of the day, you cannot deliver the legal service you are 'selling'.

To be a great lawyer, you will need to commit to learning – every day. This isn't just advice for new lawyers. If you are further down your career pathway, your learning probably extends beyond the technical aspects of your trade to include complementary skills in sales, business, marketing and leadership. You will still, of course, ensure your technical skills are being enhanced, but now your skills will be broadening. And if you are well down that law career path, I think new learning is more important than ever. It prevents us from becoming bored. Nowadays, some of my best learning comes from teaching; consider taking on a mentoring or teaching role with some of the newer lawyers around you.

If you are early on in your career, you should focus on being a great technician. Be a sponge. Learn your law and how to apply it, pay attention to everything that is happening in your firm, ask as many questions as you can, and have a go at something new whenever an opportunity arises. There are so many opportunities in big, medium and small firms for great lawyers.

Importantly, don't solely rely upon the people around you to teach you to be great; teach yourself. Don't try to become anyone else; be yourself. But do communicate with people whom you respect, whether they are inside your organisation or outside it.

In my career, I have had a handful of amazing mentors from outside where I work. These are people whom I have always been able to call on, who have given their time to me endlessly, to teach me, to show me how I can be a great lawyer, and I am eternally grateful for all of their support.

If you are starting out in this profession, find yourself four or five senior lawyers you can look up to. They might be in your practice area or they might be outside it. They might be solicitors; they might be barristers. Some of them might even be Judges. But whomever you choose, actively seek out mentors. I have found that if you are gracious and respectful, your mentors will happily give their time to you. This is a profession that, over the years, has benefitted greatly from information sharing and from mentoring, and there are senior lawyers in our profession who have so much to give. The key is to go out and find them.

Whatever area of law you have chosen to pursue, be great at it. This doesn't necessarily mean being the best at it. It means knowing your law, knowing it well, spending the time in the early part of your career submerged in reading legislation and cases, and watching those around you – not requiring them to teach you, but taking the initiative and learning regardless.

Remember that one of the best ways of learning is to make mistakes. I am not suggesting that you constantly go out there and purposefully make mistakes. We naturally want to minimise the number of mistakes we make. However, recognise that it's normal to make mistakes now and then, and that you're going to make them. When you do, it's important to learn from them and forgive yourself for them. It's important to pause and reflect upon where you went wrong so it doesn't happen again, but it's more important not to beat yourself up about it.

If you find yourself making a mistake, put your hand up early and confide in someone in your organisation – tell them sooner rather than later. That's when mistakes can easily be dealt with and resolved. It's when people sit on them, hide them and pretend they didn't happen that mistakes can become unfixable.

Being a great lawyer means building a reputation for honesty, integrity and constant learning. Those great lawyers who have been my mentors, some of whom are now Judges, are learning even now. They're still attending courses and conferences, and sitting and talking with people who have different skills and knowledge from them. They are massive sponges who never stop taking in information.

The world is changing; technology is changing. There has never been a better time to learn. So whatever stage you're at, take advantage of the times. Be a great lawyer. Make that the core of your brand and your reputation and never let that go.

HAVE COURAGE

It takes courage to be yourself in a world that is full of expectations, stereotypes and social norms. Being clear about your core values and ensuring your decisions are congruent with those values is a big step in building that courage.

Follow your intuition or 'go with your gut', as they say – it will generally lead you to 'you'. Be careful whom you surround yourself with – you need people who lift you up rather than pull you down. And don't be afraid to say 'no' when something just doesn't feel right to you.

Shakespeare famously said,

'…there is nothing either good or bad, but thinking makes it so.' We need to remember that we are both the source and the cause of our own wellbeing. Your thoughts, feelings, beliefs, values and strengths make you 'you', so why not mindfully create a life that fits with 'you' rather than fighting against it every day? I promise you the former will give you the greater chance of happiness.

Ten of my best personal attributes
*Shameless plug

1 ....

2 ....

3. ....

4. ....

5. ....

6. ....

7 ....

8 ....

9 ....

10. ....

"

Remember who you are.
Don't Allow yourself to get lost
in other people's expectations.
It's not sustainable. You are
valuable. People who know you
best will recognise your special
'flavour'. Let people see you.
that's something that makes me
incredibly motivated, and happy.

- CHRIS GRANT, GRANT AND ASSOCIATES BRISBANE -

In today's rush
we all think too much,
seek too much,
want too much
and forget about
the joy of just being

– ECKHART TOLLE –

Live life, love law and leave a legacy

You might have read this book out of curiosity, already being a very happy lawyer and just wondering what I could have to add. If that is you – great! I hope I have added or clarified something for you. Enjoy being happy and keep doing what you are doing. But if you are reading this book because you have reached a career crossroads, then this next bit is for you.

BUILD A LIFE IN THE LAW THAT YOU LOVE

Studying law and working as a lawyer, you will have learned so many wonderful skills. You could adapt them in many ways in many professions if you choose, but before you toss in the law career towel, I have a simpler suggestion for you.

Change the way you see the world. Spend a week focusing each day on seeing the good in everything, particularly the small things. To help you with this, I have a final challenge (because I love a challenge and this one involves chocolate!):

Grab two glass jars and pop them on your desk. One is the negative jar and one is the positive. Find yourself a big bag of smarties (you know, those giant ones from the supermarket). Now, let me be clear, you can't eat the smarties as we go unless they end up in the positive jar! So the challenge works like this: Every time you find yourself being negative, get drawn into a negative conversation (you know, the ones where you and your friends just complain about all the things that are wrong in life or generally gossip about others), or are just whingeing because you can, you are to take two smarties out of the bag and add them to the negative jar before putting the lid back on. You can't eat them – they are not yours! Each time you see, do, hear or think of something positive, fun, happy or joyous, take four smarties out of the bag and pop them in the positive jar. You can snack from the positive jar if you really need to, but I encourage you to try to hold off for the week and see if you can't fill it.

I am all about accountability, so if you are willing to give this challenge a go, I encourage you to bring in a friend or colleague or your partner as well. Make them do the same thing. Each of you is to hold the other accountable and ensure you are filling your jars correctly and not snacking as you go.

Do it for a week and see what happens!

We need to change how we think and what we do to change how we feel.

So start right now, and change things ...

Look after your   *Health*

Improve your   *Attitude*

Embrace your   *Passion*

Celebrate your   *Purpose*

Be   *Yourself*

Taking these steps comes down to one simple choice – choosing to be happy. Make that choice for you – not for anyone around you.

Taking these steps comes down to one simple choice – choosing to be happy. Make that choice for you – not for anyone around you.

When I was at my own career crossroads in 2013, that was really all I did. Late that Saturday night when I jumped on the computer and created 'The Happy Family Lawyer' blog, I made a decision to choose happiness. I had no idea at that time that the decision would ultimately lead to me writing this book. And I certainly had no inkling that a silly $100 website would be the beginning of me finding a true sense of happiness, not just in my law career, but in my whole life.

As you come to the end of this book, remember that while I have been talking about being a happy lawyer, and finding satisfaction, contentment and purpose in your career, I have really been encouraging you to lead a happy life. You cannot have one without the other. You are one whole person, and being happy in one aspect of your life while deeply unhappy in another will lead to unhappiness overall.

You are a person first, a lawyer second. Never forget that. Law is a career that, at times, can be so harsh, so difficult and so isolating. From one lawyer to another, I do hope we can all find ways to be kinder to one another. Sure, we might be adversaries today on some client matter, but, regardless, we are all people – people with feelings, lives, children, friends, parents and siblings. We are all people with our own struggles, just trying to do our best. As a profession, I think we can do much more to support each other. Who knows the life of a lawyer better than other lawyers?

THE FUTURE FOR THE HAPPY LAWYER

The practice of law is changing fast. Technology and offshoring are already creating significant disruption in our industry, and I expect we have much more change to come in the next few years. I encourage you to embrace the change that is occurring around you – be a part of it rather than letting it pass you by. I don't have a crystal ball and can't predict the future for our profession; however, I do think we can already see some obvious shifts occurring around us:

Smaller boutique and solo firms are now becoming the norm.

These 'micro' structures offer significant advantages to lawyers and clients alike. They are nimble, adaptable and ready to respond to change. Through technology, automation, offshoring and online resources, these micro practices are able to offer superior services to some of their 'Big Law' competitors. A micro firm also offers the happy lawyer a significant opportunity to practise in a way that is authentic to them. A small firm run by one or two lawyers will become an extension of the personalities of the people within it, so it is no surprise to me that we are seeing more and more lawyers jump ship to explore the advantages of smaller practice.

It is all about the 'niche'.

I am a Family Lawyer. However, while I can offer the whole range of Family Law services, my skill and specialty is working with clients in a way that keeps them out of the traditional Court process. Since opening my firm, I have openly marketed my practice as specialising in keeping families out of the Court process, and these past three years I have done nothing but write, speak and paint that everywhere I have gone. Now, my firm is practising almost entirely out of Court. You might think it's crazy to be saying 'No' to the viable, paying work coming through the door, but that is what we do. In fact, by being really clear on our speciality and by being the only firm for miles around actively promoting and practising in this way, we have never been busier. The 'new law' world will be full of niche firms or lawyers and I encourage you to be one of them. Play to your strengths, work out which bits of your role as a lawyer you really love and be the best at them. In turn, I'm willing to bet you improve your own happiness.

Technology is opening doors we couldn't even see before.

Technology is changing the face of everything in our lives. We can now run a law firm from the palm of our hands, and we can be virtual yet have at the tips of our fingers all the power of a big firm, thanks to outsourcing and our online world. Automation of legal services has already happened in many areas of law and no doubt this will continue at a rapid pace in the coming years. Professional services such as law are ripe for significant disruption as we have been so slow to adopt any level of change. The delivery and style of legal services is changing and we need to pay close attention to the world around us, and try new things and new ways of doing business if we don't want to be left behind.

Regardless of the trends and changes, however, remember to be true to yourself and what's really important. Despite all the factors in our profession and in our life that may change, the rewarding nature of our relationships with other people will not.

THE IMPORTANCE OF OUR RELATIONSHIPS

As human beings, we need social connection. We need friends, we need family, we need support around us. Above almost everything else, we need relationships with others. Core to human nature is a desire to be part of a community, a group, a family. In fact, our brain reacts in the same way to social rejection as it does to physical pain. Our brain is hardwired to be part of a bigger community. This is central to our survival.

My study of the science of happiness continues to show me the same thing over and over – good relationships keep us happier and healthier.

The Harvard Study of Adult Development, one of the longest running studies on human behaviour, has found that the quality of our relationships is directly connected to our health and length of life. The research from Harvard makes it really simple – good relationships (and it is quality here that really matters) keep us happier and healthier and are a key to helping us live longer.

I have learned so much in my job as a divorce lawyer, but what has really been brought home for me over and over is the importance of relationships. They are essential to our very existence and probably the most important things in our lives. Our intimate relationships, our family relationships, our relationships with our children, our relationships with our parents, our relationships with our extended family, with our friends, with our colleagues – these create those moments in life that are unforgettable.

To be truly happy, you will need to build, maintain and engage in your relationships with others.

In my job, I see the impact of relationship breakdowns on people daily, and I see many lawyers who have worked so hard to maintain their career, but at the cost of their marriage and their family.

Don't let this be you. Find a way to practise law that enables you to pursue what you want outside of law. Marriage, families and friendships are essential. They need to be given priority. Studies continually show that those of us who prioritise our relationships, particularly our family relationships, are happier.

As we move into a world of 'new law', with the boutique, smaller practices, entrepreneurial business structures and technology we've talked about, it's becoming easier and easier to think outside the box when it comes to practising law and create the lifestyle that fits with who you authentically are.

Don't be afraid to think outside the box and dream and plan and do. Create the career you want; create the career that fits who you are. If you enjoy working within a big structure, then by all means do that, but if you don't, then don't. Take the time to really think about what it is that you want to be doing with your talents in law. Don't throw out the baby with the bath water. Don't toss in the career towel. Look for friends and mentors who have found a way that works for them and see if you can't use the same tools to find a way that works for you.

LEAVING A LEGACY

Leaving a legacy means being remembered for what we have contributed to the world. Many a lawyer I have had the privilege of knowing has left a legacy worthy of the history books, but few of them will make it into those books. Rather, their great work helping others will have deeply touched the lives of many people who will remember them, and some who will never know the part they played. Every single one of us, lawyer or not, is creating part of the footprint that will become our legacy every single day.

We only have one life and it seems terribly short. I want to make my time count. I want to look back when all is said and done and be able to say to myself with confidence, 'You did it, Clarissa. You lived a life that was true to you – to what you think, feel and believe (even as those things changed over time). And you made a difference for a few others along the way. You didn't harm the world; you made it a better place for those around you.'

Most of us hope that our lives matter in some way to someone.

A happy lawyer leaves a powerful legacy. Whether it's noted in the history books or not, the work you have done today and the work you will do tomorrow is affecting someone, somewhere, in a positive way. Don't lose sight of that.

If you find your work unfulfilling, then don't be afraid to mindfully and purposefully seek out work that fulfils you. That is the beauty of law – there are so many wonderful career roads you can follow. Unless you're willing to jump on them and start driving, you'll never know which one is right for you.

HAPPY LAWYER, HAPPY LIFE; HAPPY LIFE, HAPPY LAWYER

When I was contemplating the title for this book, I played with both 'Happy lawyer, Happy life' and 'Happy life, Happy lawyer'. The order I settled on could, and perhaps should be reversed. You cannot be a happy lawyer if you are unhappy in life. Embrace the whole of your life. And embrace you for you, rather than trying to fit yourself into some sort of stereotype you have created in your own mind.

I don't profess to know what the future of our profession holds, but I am confident predicting one thing – the days of the 1980s style of aggressive lawyering are coming to an end. Next time you are firing off an email on a Saturday afternoon, I encourage you to pause and consider your colleague. Sure, they may be a battleaxe who has done nothing but bury you under nasty correspondence for the past six months, but today you have a chance to change how you work, how you think and what you do. Start with kindness, particularly towards those who might least deserve it, and you just might be surprised what happens, for them and for you.

A few years ago, I chose to be happy. Now that you are at the end of this book, I hope I have encouraged you to do the same.

I know so many great lawyers who have given up on our profession and left the traditional realms of law to find purpose and passion somewhere else. While I am all for people following their dreams and walking their own path, I am worried that too many great lawyers are leaving the traditional practice of law. Those with empathy, kindness and a desire to really leave their mark on the world are finding it easier to live their true purpose outside the constraints of traditional legal practice. There has to be another way.

Happiness is different for all of us. For me, happiness in my work came when I truly embraced being me – when I stopped worrying about what others would think and focused instead on my strengths, making time to do the things that I love and not working all of the time.

The more I have embraced just being me, running my own race and not worrying about what others may think, the happier I have become. I bring all of me to whatever I do. I am Clarissa – a wife, mother, daughter, friend, creator, writer, lover of clothes and beautiful things, athlete, designer and lawyer. I have courage, passion and drive. I am sometimes too blunt, impatient, quick to judge and very bad with detail. The list goes on, but I know my strengths and am aware of most of my limitations (although I'm sure my husband and daughter could find a few more if you ask them!). Most importantly, I know that the Clarissa you find at work will be the same one you find at home – she is just tapping into different parts of herself in larger amounts. I know that my experience as a partner, mother, daughter and friend helps me every day in the work that I do. And I also know that my experiences at work – as a divorce lawyer – help me to better understand the relationships in my life outside work. My creative self comes out everywhere and is really what makes me me. And my love of exercise, activity and health sits at the core of the energy I bring to my life and those around me.

I am a whole person with many strengths and challenges – as are you. I am not just a lawyer. Remember, you are a person first and a lawyer second.

We are lucky to be able to practise in the profession that we do. Despite all of the challenges – the crazy long hours, pressured work environments and conservative business practices – I do believe you can build a life in the law that you love.

Now you need to go out and create it.

Healthy, happy recipes

Here are some recipes to help you kick-start your health! They are from a friend of mine, Sarah Follent, the founder of Baked Livingness – look Sarah up to find many more where these came from.

bakedlivingness.com

Healthy, yummy breakfasts

for Happy Lawyers

Blueberry Dreamtime Smoothie

Ingredients

½ cucumber, chopped

½ avocado

2 tablespoons tahini

2 teaspoons carob

2 teaspoons coconut syrup

1 handful of blueberries (can be frozen)

1 cup coconut milk (I use Pureharvest Coco Quench)

Method

Gently place all ingredients together and blend until well combined. Pour into a glass and top with coconut flakes, blueberries and carob if desired.

Macca Green Apple Smoothie

Ingredients

5 macadamia nuts

1 tablespoon tahini

1 teaspoon cinnamon

2 teaspoons honey

1 green apple, chopped

1 cup coconut milk

Method

Gently place all ingredients together and blend until well combined.
Pour into a glass and top with coconut flakes, sliced apple, honey and cinnamon if desired.

Healthy, yummy snacks
for Happy Lawyers

Blueberry Dreamtime Bliss Balls
(makes 12)

This is a simple bliss ball recipe that you can get creative with and try out your own flavours. Try using dates instead of figs, goji berries instead of pumpkin seeds, almonds instead of cashews and lemon instead of blueberries. Make these on the weekend for a nourishing snack each day of the week. It is also a great idea to make them in bulk and freeze so you have a delightful snack whenever you need.

Ingredients

15 dried figs
½ cup fresh blueberries
2 tablespoons tahini
½ cup desiccated coconut
3 tablespoons coconut oil
1 cup dry roasted cashews
1 cup activated pumpkin seeds

Method

In a food processor, blend all ingredients together until well mixed and the desired texture. Work the mixture into balls using your hands. Having your hands slightly wet will help. Roll the balls into your choice of: toasted desiccated coconut, carob powder, pumpkin seeds or seed mix.

Simple Green Apple and Nut Slices

Ingredients

1 green apple
Your favourite nut or seed spread
(mine are tahini and macadamia nut butter)

Method

Cut apple into wedge-like slices.
Dip or cover top of the apple slices with your chosen nut or seed spread.
Top with goji berries, shredded coconut, cinnamon, carob nibs, activated pumpkin seeds or honey.

Green Apple & Honey Muffins

(makes 6)

This is a quick and easy muffin recipe that you can get creative with and try out your own flavours. Try using pear or strawberries instead of apple and coconut syrup or dates instead of honey. Make these on the weekend for a nourishing breakfast or afternoon tea snack each day of the week. You can double the mixture to make more and freeze.

Ingredients

2 free range eggs

¼ cup honey

¼ cup coconut milk

¼ cup coconut oil

¼ cup filtered water

1 teaspoon bicarbonate of soda

1 teaspoon cinnamon

1 vanilla bean

½ cup desiccated coconut

1 cup activated almond meal

1 green apple, grated

Method

Pre-heat oven to 180°C.

Gently place eggs, honey, coconut milk, oil, water and bicarbonate of soda into a food processor or blender.

Blend until well combined.

Add almond meal, vanilla bean, cinnamon and desiccated coconut and blend until well combined.

Stir in grated apple.

Evenly divide mixture into 6 cupcake papers.

Top with shredded coconut and apple slices if desired.

Place in oven for 30mins, checking regularly.

Allow to cool before enjoying.

Activated Seed & Zucchini Loaf

Ingredients

1 cup linseeds, freshly ground

½ cup activated almond meal

1/3 cup arrowroot flour

½ cup activated sunflower seeds, plus more for toppings

½ cup activated pumpkin seeds, plus more for toppings

1 teaspoon bi-carbonate of soda

2 teaspoons mixed herbs

4 free range eggs

1/3 cup olive oil

1/3 cup filtered water

1 zucchini, grated

Method

In a food processor, blend eggs, water, olive oil and bi-carbonate of soda until well combined.

Gently add ground linseeds, almond meal, arrowroot flour, seeds and herbs. Pulse together until combined. Some seeds should still be chunky.

Take out food processor blade and gently mix grated zucchini through.
Place in a lined loaf tin and top with additional seed.
Cover with foil and place in a 180°C oven for an hour, or until cooked.
Check and remove foil at 45mins.

Serving/ topping suggestions

Serve with your favourite nut or seed spread (I like tahini) and then top with any of the following:
- avocado, lemon, salt and pepper
- raspberries, lemon and honey
- roast veggies, basil leaves, lemon, salt and pepper
- blueberries, coconut flakes, lemon and honey
- tuna or salmon, avocado, olive oil, salt and pepper

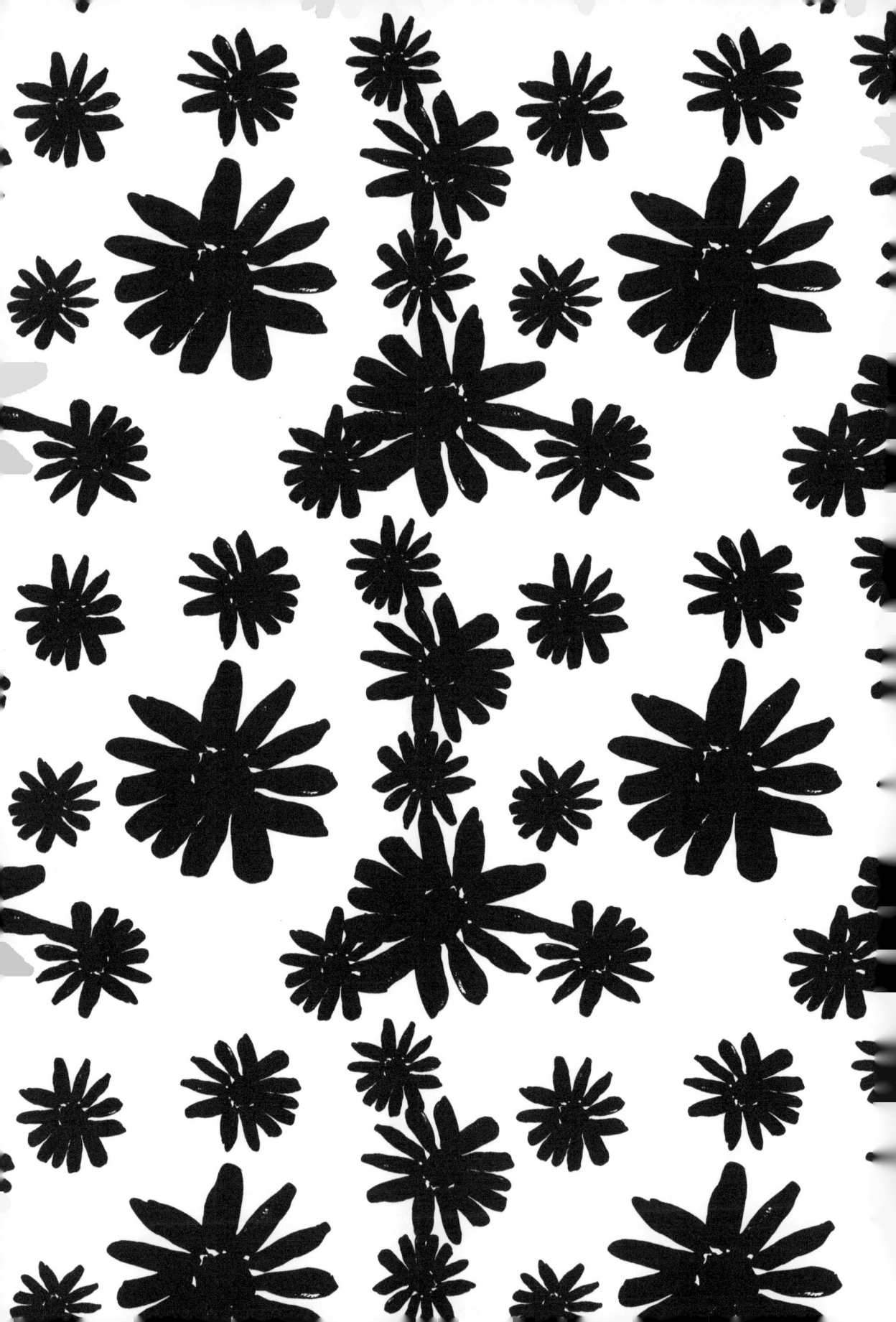

Healthy, yummy lunches

for Happy Lawyers

Baked Livingness Grilled Eggplant Wraps

Ingredients

5 large slices of grilled eggplant (these take approx 5-10mins in a grill pan, or prepare the night before)

½ beetroot grated

½ carrot grated

5 beetroot leaves, thinly sliced

Coriander

Spicy avocado and tahini dressing

Salt and pepper

Chilli to taste

Method

Place grilled eggplant on a chopping board and gently add each ingredient to each eggplant.

Top with your favourite nuts (mine are macadamias).

Add the spicy avocado and tahini dressing and wrap.

Use additional dressing as dipping sauce if required.

Spicy Avocado & Tahini Dressing

Ingredients

Juice of a small lemon
½ avocado
2 tablespoons tahini
Chilli to taste (I use 2 chillies, chopped)
2 tablespoons olive oil
2 tablespoons filtered water
Salt and pepper to taste

Method

Gently place all ingredients together and blend until well combined.
Pour over any salad or abundance bowl, use as a dipping sauce or use as dressing for my eggplant wraps.

Simple tuna & avocado sliders

Ingredients

1 x 95g tin Sirena tuna in olive oil

½ avocado

Chilli to taste

Salt and pepper

Squirt of lemon juice

½ cucumber, sliced into approx 5- 6 thick slices

1 teaspoon black sesame seeds

1 spring onion finely chopped

Method

In a bowl, add all ingredients except the cucumber and mix with a fork until well combined.

Spoon mixture onto the cucumber slices and top with additional chilli, sesame seeds and spring onion.

Avocado & Mint Salsa Lettuce Cups

Ingredients

6-8 cos lettuce leaves

½ avocado

½ cucumber

½ capsicum

10 mint leaves, finely chopped

Juice of a small lemon

2 tablespoons olive oil

Salt and pepper

Chilli to taste

Method

Chop avocado, cucumber and capsicum into small cubes.

In a bowl, mix in mint, lemon juice, olive oil, chilli, salt and pepper.

Spoon mixture into washed cos lettuce leaves.

Top with your favourite seeds and nuts.

Experiment and get creative with different herbs and vegetables.

Baked Livingness Vibrant Green Bowl

Ingredients

½ zucchini, sliced with a julienne peeler

Leaves of two kale stems

Lemon

Olive oil

½ avocado

½ cucumber, chopped into cubes

1 piece of celery, thinly chopped

1 tablespoon activated pumpkin seeds

2 teaspoons zested avocado seed

Salt and pepper

Spicy avocado and tahini dressing

Method

Massage kale in lemon juice and olive oil. Leave to sit while you prepare other ingredients. Delicately place zucchini, kale, cucumber, celery and avocado in a bowl. Season bowl with salt and pepper to your liking. Top with pumpkin seeds, zested avocado seed, spicy avocado and tahini dressing.

Baked Livingness Sushi

Ingredients

1 cucumber

3-4 pieces of smoked salmon diced

½ red onion, finely sliced

2 tablespoons spicy avocado and tahini dressing

1 teaspoon sesame seeds

½ carrot, finely diced

½ avocado

Salt and pepper

Method

Cut the cucumber into even 2cm-thick rolls.

With a small, sharp knife, carefully remove the flesh and seed part of the cucumber, keeping the 'walls' intact. In a bowl, mix all other ingredients together until mixture comes together. Fill the cucumber rings with salmon and avocado mixture. Press the mixture down well to ensure that it will remain in place. Top with additional sesame seeds.

Acknowledgements

Happy Lawyer, Happy Life started out as a bit of a passion project of mine. Initially I questioned whether my own experience in law and life could really be of use to anyone else, but now I am hopeful that it can.

There are so many people who, each day, through their kindness, support and care, make my life a little easier, and there are some whom I would particularly like to thank here.

I would like to thank my friends, family and colleagues who have put up with endless questions, note-taking during our conversations, and weekend trips interrupted by my musings on life, law and happiness.

To **Melissa Nielsen** and **Melissa Telecican**, thank you for your ongoing support as my closest friends and for putting up with the whirlwind that is the mind of Clarissa.

To **Fiona Caulley**, **Anne-Marie Rice** and **Hayley Cunningham**, your kindness and openness as we share our experiences has inspired so much of this book. I will be forever grateful for such deep friendships that have come thanks to my life in law.

To **Debbie Ryan**, my 'person' at work, who does so much for me and everyone else and supports all of my crazy ideas (even when they turn our lives upside down) – thank you. Who could have imagined that our law journey together would take us where it has!

To **Amelia** and **Marshall Rees**, thank you for your support, always, in so many ways, and, of course, Marshall, for your beautiful image for the book.

To **Sarah** and **Kate Follent**, the kindness, support and ongoing friendship you give me, London and Ollie will never be forgotten.

To **my team** at BFLC, particularly **Freya, Charles, Laura, Kobi, Hayley, Loreena** and **Jo**, and all of the new additions – thank you for inspiring me, every day, to follow my dreams (and keep my office running as I do!).

To my mentors in law and in life – **Jen McArdle, Rob Grant, Justice Colin Forrest, Ann Harper, Jacoba Brasch QC** – thank you for all you have done for me in my career. I only hope I can give back to others half as much as you have all so generously given to me.

And, most importantly, thank you to my parents, **Jane** and **Forster**; my husband, **Oliver**; and my daughter, **London**, who teach me every single day the value of my life and provide so much of my happiness.

Thank you.

About the Author

Clarissa Rayward practises as a Divorce Lawyer in Brisbane, Queensland, Australia, where she is the Director of the boutique specialist family law firm, Brisbane Family Law Centre.

Clarissa is a wife and mum who is passionate about relationships, people and family. She is using her industry knowledge and skill to change the way Australian families experience divorce and separation. She is known as 'The Happy Family Lawyer' because she believes that your divorce can be something you can look back on with pride.

In 2013, Clarissa started writing her thoughts on how to have a 'happy divorce' on a simple blog called 'The Happy Family Lawyer'. What began as her weekly ramblings has fast become a popular resource centre for families navigating the legal aspects of their divorce and separation, who are seeking an amicable and dignified divorce.

In 2015, Clarissa published her first book, Splitsville – How to separate, stay out of Court and stay friends – a resource for separating families.

Clarissa's own story of finding happiness in her legal career has inspired this new direction and this book. Clarissa is now determined to be an active part of the dialogue encouraging lawyers to consider better ways of finding balance, health and longevity in their careers.

In 2016, Clarissa launched the 'Happy Lawyer, Happy Life' podcast in response to the growing number of lawyers and other professionals reaching out to her and looking for ways of finding 'Happiness' in their careers. Each week, Clarissa interviews a lawyer with a compelling story and taps into how other lawyers balance life, law and happiness in their careers.

Clarissa is regularly called upon to present to family lawyers and other professionals on matters relating to law, life and business.

CONNECT WITH CLARISSA BY:

Phone: (+61) 73862 1955

Email: clarissa@thehappyfamilylawyer.com

Website: www.thehappyfamilylawyer.com

www.brisbanefamilylawcentre.com.au

Facebook: www.facebook.com/thehappyfamilylawyer

Instagram: www.instagram.com/thehappyfamilylawyer

Twitter: www.twitter.com/clarissarayward

www.ingramcontent.com/pod-product-compliance
Lightning Source LLC
Chambersburg PA
CBHW051659210326
41597CB00034B/6177